THE AMERICAN BEAVER IN NEW YORK (1895-2005)

A Century of Wildlife Conservation

ROBERT F. GOTIE AND MARK K. BROWN

DORRANCE
PUBLISHING CO
EST. 1920
PITTSBURGH, PENNSYLVANIA 15238

The contents of this work, including, but not limited to, the accuracy of events, people, and places depicted; opinions expressed; permission to use previously published materials included; and any advice given or actions advocated are solely the responsibility of the author, who assumes all liability for said work and indemnifies the publisher against any claims stemming from publication of the work.

Dorrance Publishing Co
585 Alpha Drive
Pittsburgh, PA 15238
Visit our website at *www.dorrancebookstore.com*

ISBN: 978-1-6393-7254-6
eISBN: 978-1-6393-7636-0

The American Beaver in New York (1895-2005)

*"A Statement before made may be here repeated,
that the beaver, with his life, has contributed in no small degree to
the colonization and settlement of the
British Provinces and the United States".*
Lewis Henry Morgan,
***The American Beaver and his Works,* 1868**

*"From the evidence of their passing, they seem to have completely
possessed the land and to have been abundant beyond our present
conception".*
Harry V. Radford,
***History of the Adirondack Beaver,* 1907.**

CONTENTS

Tables
Table 1. Beaver releases in the Adirondacks (1901-1909).
Table 2. Estimated Value of Wild Fur Harvested in NY (1980 – 1998).
Table 3. Trapping License Sales in New York 1940-2003
Table 4. Beaver Population Statistics for the Appalachian Plateau in Central New York
Table 5. Relative Trapper Income as a function of the decline in the value of the US dollar
Table 6. Percent of Active Beaver Colonies that become Beaver Problems in New York.
Table 7. Types of Beaver Problems in upstate NY DEC Regions. (1990-1997)

Illustrations
Figure 1. New York beaver population (1800 -2002).
Figure 2. The Village of Old Forge was a location where beavers were released in 1904-05.
Figure 3. The first pelt seals were of a metal design.
Figure 4. Early aerial survey used in the Adirondacks and Tug Hill from (1954-1980).
Figure 5. 2x3mi. aerial survey plots became the statewide norm after 1992.
Figure 6. Aerial survey of several active beaver ponds in 3 Rivers WMA-Baldwinsville, NY.

Figure 25. A sample of plastic pelt tags used between (1984-2001).

Figure 26. Furbearer possession cards were used to gather information on the harvest.

Figure 27. Multiple beaver possession report card developed in the 1990's.

Figure 28. Average annual number of beavers harvested in New York (1930's -2000's).

Figure 29. The purchasing power of a beaver pelt in the last quarter of the 20th Century.

Figure 30. Total value and the harvest of all furbearer species in New York (1980-1998).

Figure 31. Trappers using the "Beaver Bus" released hundreds of beavers between (1932-38).

Figure 32. Electric shockers as a preventive measure at road culverts did not prove reliable.

Figure 33. The deep-water fence helped to guard road culverts from beaver activity.

Figure 34. This pond leveler failed after a few weeks when beaver built a dam downstream.

Figure 35. Serious damage to the future Adirondack RR caused by beaver activity (1975).

Figure 36. Survey along the Adirondack Railway – 1975.

Figure 37. Average annual number of beaver -human conflicts in New York (1940's - 2000's).

FOREWORD

"The status of beavers (<u>Castor canadensis</u>) in New York has changed many times in the last three centuries, as have people's attitudes towards the American Beaver. Beavers have always held some value to people, whether as religious objects, sources of food, clothing or as amazing animals. Beavers, however, have also caused problems with their tree cutting and dam building activities; at least since the arrival of Europeans whose culture included property ownership. Whether the positive or negative value of beaver has always been fully understood is still unclear today. The species has seldom been treated in a balanced way that would indicate such an understanding. Rather, this interest or that has prevailed over the centuries resulting in quite different actions as the beaver's status changed in New York.

"We exploited beavers when doing so was profitable in the short term. Then we mourned their loss and sought to restore them to the state. We quickly learned that they could cause problems to people, but since the protectionist tide was high, we moved them to other areas rather than kill them; seemingly oblivious to the lesson just learned. Or, perhaps some of those early decision makers understood that they had a beneficial side.

"By the time beavers inhabited most of the state, our decision makers recognized we valued them for fur at least, because we managed them for sustained yield where there were no conflicts with agriculture. Some early wildlife biologists understood the dual nature of beavers beyond their pelt value, but decision makers at the time did not reflect this understanding. Concrete recognition of beavers beyond fur value only came in the last quarter of the 20th Century. It came from a handful of New York regional wildlife biologists with the vision to see the promise of actually managing a key stone species throughout New York."

Bishop, P. G. 1987. Introduction. In: Robert F. Gotie, E. Michael Ermer, Mark K. Brown and Paul G. Bishop. Progress in Beaver Management in New York State. Unpublished manuscript. NYS DEC, Bureau of Wildlife, Cortland, NY, 12/30/87.

INTRODUCTION

New York's contemporary story about the most important furbearing mammal in its history formally began in 1987 in the form of a narrative that evolved four years later into a wide-ranging statewide management plan for the American beaver. The story unfolds now, after 30 years of collecting dust, as a mostly complete historical account of New York's effort to manage beavers during the 20th century. It is told here by two wildlife biologists who played a direct and vital role in managing the American beaver during the last quarter of the 1900s.

As the 21st century moves forward, the chapters that follow will describe the steps taken to purposely return and eventually increase the American beaver from none to many during the 20th century in New York State. It is likely, however, the management philosophy that prevailed during this century will not survive the next generation of management thought, just as the 18th and 19th century viewpoint was swept aside in the 1890s.

With all historical narratives, authors must sometimes interpret observations already filtered through the eyes of people merely on the side lines of events. As actual participants in this story between 1972 and 2005, we have included relevant internal correspondence and unpublished reports found only in the files still available in regional wildlife offices. We apologize for any omissions, errors or misinterpretations that we may have made while preparing this narrative.

Note: The agency charged with the responsibility to manage resources in New York State has changed names many times in its 152-year history. The authors have referred to the agency by its appropriate name at the time of the occasion being described. The chronology of names is as follows:

1868 New York State Fisheries Commission
1885 New York State Forest Commission
1895 New York State Forest, Fish and Game Commission
1911 New York State Conservation Commission
1926 New York State Conservation Department
1970 New York State Department of Environmental Conservation

CHAPTER I

PROTECTION AND RESTORATION
(1895–1923)

Prior Status

The American beaver was nearly extirpated from the North American continent in less than two centuries, because of their abundance and economic importance. [1] Indiscriminate exploitation was the root cause. At the end of the 19th century, Harry V. Radford in his influential report to the New York State Legislature concluded the American beaver was essentially extirpated in New York by the end of the 19th Century. (**Figure 1**) He personally knew of only one active beaver colony in 1894 located in Township 20, south and west of St. Regis Mountain. [2] Since then, much has been done by many states to return this species to a prominent role in the environmental health of our nation. Likewise, New York State played an especially historical and pivotal role in this endeavor. Not only was New York the first state to re-establish this species early in the 20th century, it was the first state to use the beaver's pond building activity as an important element in its statewide wetland management program.

Legislation

The historical record on the American beaver prior to 1800 is incomplete. However, New York's total beaver population in 1609 was sug-

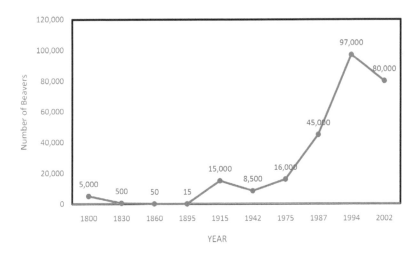

Figure 1. New York beaver population (1800-2002)

1800 to 1895 estimates taken from Harry V. Radford 1907. History of the Adirondack Beaver. Annual Reports, NYS Forest,

Fish and Game Commission: 1904, 1905 & 1906.

1915 estimate taken from 18th Annual Report of the NY Conservation Commission, 1928.

1942 estimate taken from 32nd Annual Report of the NY Conservation Department, 1942.

1975 estimate taken from Paul G. Bishop et. al. 1992. Beaver Management in New York State.

1987 estimate taken from Robert F. Gotie et.al. 1988. Progress in Beaver Management.

1994 estimate taken from Gordon Batcheller 1995. The 1995 Update on the NYS Beaver management Program.

2002 estimate taken from Robert F. Gotie 2004. NY Statewide Beaver Data Summary.

gested to be between one million and three million animals. [3] [4] "*While the indigenous people of New York had little impact on the abundant beaver population in New York at this time, the struggle for control of the New World fur trade by European powers in the forepart of the seventeenth century marked the beginning of the end for the American Beaver.*" [5] It was clear that in the last decade of the 19th century the American Beaver was essentially extinct in New York State. [6]

Recognition that the American Beaver was gone from the New York landscape was part of a national awakening. "*The national mood at the turn of the 20th century was that we either stopped exploiting our wildlife resources or nothing would be left.*" [7] Conservation was needed. This vision for the new century was reflected in the landmark Act of June 7, 1895. Chapter 974, Article III, section 50 of the New York Fisheries, Game and Forest Law clearly articulated the new will of the people, "*No beaver shall be caught or killed at any time in this state.*" "*Whoever shall violate or attempt to violate the provisions of this section shall be deemed guilty of a misdemeanor, and in addition thereto shall be liable to penalty of 50 dollars for each beaver caught or killed in violation of this section.*" [8]

In 1904, the law was broadened to prohibit disturbing beaver dams and houses as well, "*No trap, snare, pit, dead fall or other device to entrap or entice beaver shall be made, set or used, nor shall beaver be taken by aid or use thereof.*" "*No person shall molest or disturb any wild beaver at the dams, houses, homes or abiding places of same.*" [9] Although restrictions on trap placement traces its roots to this 1904 law, in 1950 the original law was amended to more clearly define the prohibitions on setting and staking traps on or near beaver houses or dams. It stated, "*No person shall disturb a beaver dam, den or house at any time, nor set, stake or use a trap within a distance of 15 feet of such house, dam or den, **except as permitted by the Department.**"* [10] The intended purpose was to better protect beaver houses, dams and dens from disturbance by trappers and to better protect the beaver resource. [11] Over the last 50 years of the 20th century, the exception clause to this law has been repeatedly exercised and reinstated to both protect beavers and river otters from excessive trapping mortality.

Figure 2. The Village of Old Forge was a location where beavers were released in 1904-05.

Beaver Releases

Between 1904 and 1906, through the political influence of concerned citizens, a total of $1,500 was appropriated by the State Legislature for the purchase and release of beavers. Several wealthy individuals also acquired beaver for release on their Adirondack estates. Between 1901 and 1907, 35 beavers from Ontario, Canada and Yellowstone Park, Wyoming were released in the Adirondacks.

Beginning in 1901, Edward Litchfield released twelve beavers on his preserve on Big Tupper Lake. In 1902 a beaver escaped from Timothy Woodruff's preserve and took up residence at the mouth of Sumner Stream near Old Forge, NY. The Forest Fish and Game Commission then released 6 beavers in 1905. (**Figure 2**) Two were released at the junction of Sumner Stream and the south branch of the Moose River and four were set free in Big Moose Lake. The Honorable George Stevens in 1906 liberated one beaver at Lake Placid. While that same year the state released fourteen more beaver: eight in the Fulton Chain (near First and Fourth Lakes), four on the outlet of Lake Terror in Township Forty-Two, and two in Little Tupper Lake.

Table 1. Beaver Releases in the Adirondacks (1901-1909)

Agency/Person	Year	Number
Edward H. Litchfield	1901	12
Timothy Woodruff	1902	1
New York State Forest Fish and Game Commission	1905	6*
George Stevens	1906	1
New York State Forest Fish and Game Commission	1906	14**
New York State Forest Fish and Game Commission	1909	1
Total		35

* Part of the Canadian Exhibit at the Louisiana Purchase Expo
** Part of the Yellowstone Park consignment
Note: Beaver Release Summary taken from New York's 11th and 16th Annual Report of Forest, Fish and Game Commission.

The state set free one last beaver from a total of 21 in all at Lake Placid in 1909. (**Table 1**) These releases and complete protection from human exploitation allowed the beaver population to increase to an estimated 100 animals by the end of 1907. [12]

Conflict in Values

Between 1907 and 1913, the beaver population and its distribution continued to increase in the Adirondack and Lower Catskill Mountain Regions. [13] The beavers found in Orange County (Lower Catskills) were suspected to have migrated from the preserve of Rutherford Stuyvesant at Allamuchy, New Jersey. None of the original 35 beavers released in New York were transplanted anywhere near the counties encompassing the Catskill Mountains.

Although beavers were still viewed favorably by most people, the New York State Conservation Commission recognized that the beaver's return was not without peril. In 1911 the Conservation Commission, *"put up a 100-rod fine woven wire fence on the property of*

Dr. Nicoll's Camp in the vicinity of Old Forge and 40 rods on land owned by Mr. DeCamp to prevent the beavers from cutting trees." [14]

People's attitudes about beavers were still very positive and supportive of full protection in 1912, but by 1915 the Conservation Commission saw the need to remove some beavers when it involved damage to private property. Beavers had become so numerous by then that the state began occasionally issuing permits for dynamiting dams and houses to persons suffering damage. [15] This departure from full protection for beavers and their dams was made possible in 1912 by passage of the Conservation Law of New York State, Chapter 318. [16] This law authorized the Conservation Commission to permit the taking of protected animals that had become destructive to public or private property. As early as 1913, the possibility of a trapping season was first considered due to the continued increase in the beaver population and subsequent problems associated with beaver activity. [17]

In spite of efforts to provide private landowners the legal ability to solve their issues with beavers, William G. Barret successfully sued the state in 1916 for damages to his property caused by beavers cutting trees and flooding his land. This judgement was reversed in a landmark decision in 1917 by New York's highest court, the State Court of Appeals. [18] The Court of Appeals essentially said that damage to private property by beavers was basically an act of God. This decision absolved the state from future liability for damages to property caused by wildlife. The Barret decision was reaffirmed in 1962 when the New York State Court of Appeals heard the case of Crissafulli vs New York. [19] However, the Justices further stipulated that once the state recognizes property damage by beavers, they are obligated to provide a means (ministerial action) of eliminating or mitigating the damages in a timely fashion.

A formal survey of the Adirondack Park forest lands by New York's Forest Ranger staff in 1919 found beaver dams flooding 8,681 acres of timber worth about $5,425. [20] Furthermore, two thirds of these flooded lands were on State Forest Preserve. In 1920, the Conservation Commission directed game protectors and forest rangers to destroy beaver dams and houses in certain situations involving damage to timber. That same year, for the first time, 53 nuisance beavers were reported killed on permits issued by the Conservation Commission. [21]

By 1922 the Conservation Commission recognized that simply destroying dams and lodges and issuing permits to landowners to trap beaver would not control the increasing number of problems for long. The truth of this recognition took 75 years before it was mathematically proven in 1997 by Michael Runge, a doctoral candidate at Cornell University. In a mathematical analysis of New York's existing beaver damage program for the NYS Furbearer Management Team he found, *"nuisance control will not ever be large enough to have a regulatory effect. Removal of a greater number of beavers from the population would be needed, more so then removing a small number of beavers from problem locations."* [22]

A request for authority to open a limited trapping season with the goal of controlling beaver population growth and reducing damage to timber, roads, docks, waterways and aesthetics was thus submitted to the New York State Legislature. Many Adirondack Forest Preserve advocates felt that the beaver was a *"nuisance"* and that *"the problem of timber damage must receive serious attention in connection with protecting our Adirondack Forests."* [23] Chapter 308 of the Conservation Laws of 1923, passed by the State Legislature, finally authorized the Conservation Commission to allow the limited taking of beaver by a regulated trapping season. [24] The beaver at this time became the only game species whereby the Commission was uniquely empowered to declare open seasons and bag limits. Season regulations for all other species, defined as game species, resided with the State Legislature.

At the time, public sentiment regarding the need to trap beavers to control damage was predictably divided. Those not experiencing property damage and with protectionist attitudes strongly favored complete protection of beavers. Those experiencing property damage were unanimously opposed to further protection. Given the numerous damage complaints reported to the Conservation Commission, the New York State Legislature felt that complete protection was no longer justified. [25]

References

[1] C. Hart Merriam 1886. The Mammals of the Adirondack Region, 318pp.

[2] Harry V. Radford 1907. History of the Adirondack Beaver. Annual Report NYS Forest, Fish and Game Commission for 1904, 1905, 1906, pp 389-418.

[3] Charles H. Willoughby 1920. Beavers and the Adirondacks. NY Conservationist Volume III Number 5: 67-70.

[4] Harry V. Radford 1907. op. cit.

[5] Charles H. Willoughby 1920. op. cit.

[6] Frederick C. Paulmier 1903. The Squirrels and Other Rodents of the Adirondacks. 8th Report of the Forest, Fish and Game Commission.

[7] John Madison and Edward Kosicky 1971. Game, Gunners and Biology – The Scientific Approach to Wildlife Management. Conservation Dept. Winchester-Western Division, Olin Corp., Winchester Press, East Alton, IL, 48pp.

[8] 1st Annual Report of the Commissioners of Fisheries, Game and Forests, New York 1911. 1904, 1905, 1906 pp 389-418.

[9] Harry V. Radford 1907. op. cit.

[10] Conservation Law of New York, Chapter 180, p 701.

[11] Letter from Perry B. Duryea to the Honorable L.E. Walsh, 1950.

[12] James S. Whipple, Commissioner, Forest Fish and Game Commission. 11th & 16th Annual Report to the NY Legislature, 1907 and 1910, respectively.

[13] James S. Whipple, Commissioner, Forest, Fish and Game Commission. 16th Annual Report to the NY Legislature, 1910.

[14] 1st Annual Report of the Conservation Commission 1911. op. cit.

[15] 6th Annual Report of the Conservation Commission New York, 1916.

[16] 3rd Annual Report of the Conservation Commission New York, 1913.

[17] 3rd Annual Report 1913. op. cit.

[18] Barret vs State of New York Court of Appeals, 220 NY 423, 1917.

[19] Crisafulli vs State of New York Court of Appeals, 322 NY, 1971.

[20] 9th Annual Report of the Conservation Commission New York, 1919.

[21] 10th Annual Report of the Conservation Commission New York, 1920.

[22] Michael C. Runge 1997. Nuisance Beaver Analysis. Presentation given to the New York State Department of Environmental Conservation, Fur-

bearer Management Team, PhD Candidate, Cornell University, Ithaca, NY, USA, 22 May 1997.

[23] 12th Annual Report of the Conservation Commission New York, 1922.

[24] 13th Annual Report of the Conservation Commission New York, 1923.

[25] 13th Annual Report 1923. op. cit.

CHAPTER II

RETURN OF BEAVER TRAPPING

Early Trapping Seasons

The first open season for trapping beaver after 29 years of protection was held from March 1 to March 31, 1924. [1] The season was opened in nine Adirondack counties (Hamilton, Essex, Warren, Saratoga, Fulton, Clinton, Franklin, St Lawrence, Herkimer) and part of Lewis County. This same season and open trapping area repeated in 1925. [2] It was estimated that at least 2,500 and 3,600 beavers were taken during 1924 and 1925, respectively. [3]

Staff of the Roosevelt Wildlife Forest Experiment Station (at Syracuse University, College of Forestry, now State University of New York, College of Environmental Science and Forestry) severely criticized the Conservation Commission for their serious lack of effort to accurately record the harvest of this valuable furbearing mammal. Charles E. Johnson, a researcher at the Roosevelt Station, recommended mandatory pelt tagging to obtain an accurate record of the beaver harvest. [4] No further open trapping seasons were held in 1926 and 1927, because beaver damage complaints significantly declined. It should be noted, a fur trapping license requirement was added in 1927 (Section 185), which actually re-codified the laws of 1908 authorizing a hunting license. [5] The next open season, in 1928, was similar to the 1924 and 1925 seasons in timing and area. Like the first two seasons, no effort was made to obtain an accurate accounting of the harvest. Instead, the Commission estimated a harvest of 5,000 beaver, with an average pelt value of $40.00. [6]

Trapping Season Controversies

The five years following the close of the 1928 season represented the *"high tide"* of favorable public sentiment toward beaver. [7] Charles E. Johnson best described the mood of many people in the Adirondacks when he wrote, *"Not that there may frequently be justification for complaints against activities of beaver, but for myself, in light of the violent clamor that has been raised against beaver in recent years, has been prompted more by prejudice and selfish interest than by real cause or grievance."* [8] In his study of the Adirondack Beaver he logically exposed the weakness of the Conservation Department's analysis that led to the first open trapping season. He stated, *"It is difficult to avoid the impression that the compiler of the statistics on timber damage has been extravagant in the use of the figures."* *"It seems to be straining the point rather severely to place such astonishing monetary value upon a commodity which, even if it had not been damaged or destroyed by beaver flows, could not have been taken off or sold or otherwise realized upon, because of constitutional prohibition."* [9]

It seems likely Mr. Johnson's unfavorable article published in a prestigious journal of the time, influenced the New York State Legislature to change the makeup of the Conservation Department. In 1931 the State Legislature created the Bureau of Game Management within the Conservation Department to presumably provide a more scientific basis for managing beaver populations. [10] Perhaps these criticisms also precipitated a renewed popularity for beavers by the wealthy class of the Adirondacks, resulting in political pressure brought on the Conservation Department. All the same, from 1928 to 1933 the trapping season for beaver remained closed. Predictably this caused a dramatic rise in beaver damage complaints. [11]

The trapping season reopened in 1934 to again control beaver damage problems. At the time beavers were rapidly expanding their distribution outside of the Adirondack Region. Three Counties (Orange, Rockland and Sullivan) were opened that year for the first time since 1895. [12] The 1934 season included only the last two weeks in March, rather than all of March, as before. Furthermore, each trapper could take only six beavers per season. For the first time, trappers were also required to submit their pelts to a game protector or forest ranger for official tagging. [13] Similar rules prevailed through the years 1935 to 1957, as the Department expanded beaver trapping seasons throughout most of New York. Seasonal bag-limits were dropped in the Adirondacks in 1953. [14] and in the rest of the State in 1968. [15]

Except for 1947, 22 annual trapping seasons were held between 1941 and 1964. [16] Several changes in trapping regulations occurred during this period. In 1955, the entire state with the exception of New York City and Long Island was open to beaver trapping for the first time, indicating that beavers were well distributed throughout New York. [17] The first fall seasons were held in 1958, effectively expanding the amount of time trappers could legally take beaver for their pelts. [18] A half century after releasing beavers in the state to restore an extirpated species, it was now clear that by 1958 beavers were now a common mammal throughout New York.

Shortly after the beaver trapping season was opened, a mild controversy arose within the scientific and trapper fraternity. Trappers began to complain about lightly colored beaver pelts which they considered inferior *"yellow beaver."* [19] In a publication written for the Conservation Department and the New York State College of Forestry in 1935, Gurth Whipple wrote, *"It is unfortunate that many beavers inhabiting New York today have pelts which are markedly inferior to our native black beaver."* [20] Some of the earliest translocated beaver emanated from Wyoming where beaver pelts are indeed paler than those from their Ontario counterparts and other eastern sections. [21] Thus, the NYS Conservation Department was blamed for mixing inferior animals into the beaver population gene pool. Indeed, during the early years of an organized effort by the NY Bureau of Game to translocate nuisance beavers across the state, state trappers were ordered to kill "yellow beavers" rather than transfer them to other parts of New York. [22]

It is important to note that concerns about hybridization of the same species from different ecosystems in translocation programs involving other species persisted in the minds of trappers even as late as the 1990s. In 1994 and again in 1997 the NY Bureau of Wildlife contemplated the possibility of buying river otters from North Carolina and Louisiana when the NY River Otter Project of the late 1990s was failing to meet its, objective of releasing 270 otters by the year 2000.

The otters for this major Citizen Science project were being obtained from trained and licensed trappers in the Adirondack and Catskill regions. Some New York trappers from western NY, who were members of the NY River Otter Project, fell back on their earlier belief about yellow beavers. They strongly opposed the NY Bureau of Wildlife buying river otters from another state. They believed doing so would result in a hybrid otter unable to withstand the rigors of New York's environment and produce inferior pelts for trappers to sell once they were well established. At the urging of the lead author, New York's Chief Wildlife Biologist Gary Parsons solved this dilemma by doubling the price the agency was paying New York trappers to provide healthy live otters for translocation. With an infusion of more money from New York's Federal Aid in Wildlife Restoration Program, the NY River Otter Project was able to complete the restoration of river otters on time and the NY Bureau of Wildlife no longer needed to consider buying otters from another state.

Even though there was some early progress made in beaver management during the 1940s, a major shift in program emphasis from species management to active manipulation of wetland habitat halted further growth for nearly two decades. During the 1950s through the 1970s setting of trapping seasons seemed to be driven by a need to control Bureau of Wildlife expenses directed towards resolving beaver damage complaints.

Mid Century Trapping Seasons

Trapping seasons in the 1950s through the 1970s were rarely shortened or lengthened, nor their timing changed over these years. In much of New York the static nature of the trapping seasons produced prolonged over-harvests and subsequent low isolated beaver populations. The dynamic nature of the fur market thus became the only driving mechanism in New York's beaver management program. The NY Bureau of Wildlife, especially the regional wildlife offices at the time, were perfectly happy with the status quo. As long as beaver damage complaints were kept to an acceptable low level, there was no need to do anything more. When the wildlife office in the southeastern Adirondacks began to examine the effect of trapping on beaver populations in the 1970s, most of the eight other wildlife managers scoffed at these studies and some even considered them merely hobby projects of biologists with too much time on their hands. (personal communication to the lead author in 1974 from Stuart Cameron, Region 6 Wildlife Manager)

From 1958 to 1980 a variety of different trapping seasons existed throughout New York, and they generally included the days between December and March. In the northern portion of the state, beaver trapping was allowed on beaver dams, but prohibited in southern and western New York. For unknown reasons, trapping on dams was allowed statewide between 1959 and 1965. Beginning in 1965, trapping on beaver dams was sometimes prohibited and sometimes allowed in southern and western New York, presumably the result of organized trapper influence on wildlife field office managers. For the most part, wildlife managers were uninformed about the effect trapping seasons had on beaver populations. Hence, they usually deferred to the wishes of trapper organizations when setting rules and regulations. The River Otter Restoration Project began in 1995. Wildlife biologists directly involved with this project, concerned about accidental otter mortality in traps set for beavers, soon succeeded in reestablishing the prohibition for setting traps on and near beaver dams. It was one small step taken to reduce unwanted otter mortality that would be followed by a bigger step to make the most widely used beaver trap more selective.

Early Harvest Record Keeping

Trappers were first required in 1934 to submit their beaver pelts to a game protector or forest ranger for official tagging, after the season

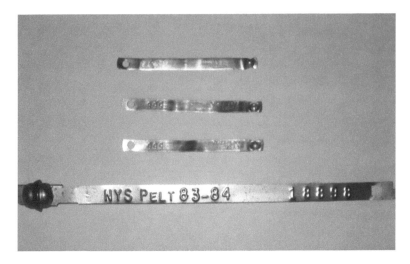

Figure 3. The first pelt seals were of a metal design.

closed and before they could be transferred or sold. At first tagging of pelts involved attaching a metal seal, (**Figure 3**) which was fixed on each pelt by the officer and tallied by county. Tagging beaver pelts this way provided an accurate census of the annual legal beaver harvest and dissuaded trappers from illegally taking and then selling ill-gotten beaver pelts. The procedure was modified in 1937 to account for the number of trappers taking beaver in each open county. Pelt tagging in this manner continued from 1937 until 1959-60. [23] For some unknown reason it was discontinued from 1960-61 through 1965-66. [24] [25] Re-organization of the Wildlife and Law Enforcement Bureau's within the Conservation Department may have been the reason behind this lack of interest in beaver management at this time. Unfortunately, no information on beaver harvest was collected during these five years. Pelt-tagging resumed again for the 1966-67 season, guided by the Bureau of Game and subsequently the Bureau of Wildlife. [26] It continued in a similar format with significant procedural changes until the end of the 2009-2010 trapping season when sealing of beaver pelts at the close of the trapping season was completely eliminated. [27] (**Appendix 1**)

References

[1] 14th Annual Report of the Conservation Commission New York, 1924.

[2] 15th Annual Report of the Conservation Commission New York, 1925.

[3] Charles E. Johnson 1927. The Beaver in the Adirondacks. Roosevelt Wildlife Bulletin, Vol. 4 (4), pp569-581.

[4] Charles E. Johnson 1927. op. cit.

[5] 17th Annual Report of the Conservation Department New York, 1927.

[6] 18th Annual Report of the Conservation Department New York, 1928.

[7] Gardiner Bump and Arthur H. Cook 1941. Black Gold – The Story of Beaver in New York State. NYS Fish and Game Management Bulletin No. 2.

[8] Charles E. Johnson 1927. op. cit.

[9] Charles E. Johnson 1927. op. cit.

[10] 21st Annual Report of the Conservation Department New York, 1931.

[11] 23rd Annual Report of the Conservation Department New York, 1933.

[12] 24th Annual Report of the Conservation Department New York, 1934.

[13] 24th Annual Report 1934. op. cit.

[14] 42nd Annual Report to the Legislature, Conservation Department New York 1952.

[15] 58th Annual Report to the Legislature, Conservation Department New York 1968.

[16] Gardiner Bump 1947. A Breather for the Beaver. NYS Conservationist Magazine, Vol. 5, pp 7-9.

[17] 45th Annual Report to the Legislature, Conservation Department New York, 1955.

[18] 48th Annual Report to the Legislature, Conservation Department New York, 1958.

[19] Gardiner Bump and Arthur Cook 1941. op. cit.

[20] Gurth Whipple 1935. Fifty Years of Conservation in New York State 1885-1935. NY State Conservation Department and NY State College of Forestry Publication.

[21] Martyn E. Obbard 1987. Fur Grading and Pelt Identification. In Wild Furbearer Management and Conservation in North America. Edited by M. Novak et. al., Ministry of Natural Resources, Ontario, 1150 pp.

[22] Gardiner Bump and Arthur Cook 1941. op. cit.

[23] W. Mason Lawrence 1959. Hunting, Trapping and Fishing Syllabus for 1959-60. NYS Conservation Department, Division of Fish & Wildlife, Albany, NY, USA.

[24] W. Mason Lawrence 1960. Hunting, Trapping and Fishing Syllabus for 1960-61. NYS Conservation Department, Division of Fish & Wildlife, Albany, NY, USA.

[25] E. L. Cheatum 1965. Hunting, Trapping and Fishing Syllabus 1965-66. NYS Conservation Department, Division of Fish & Wildlife, Albany, NY, USA.

[26] E. L. Cheatum 1966. Hunting, Trapping and Fishing Syllabus 1966-67. NYS Conservation Department, Division of Fish & Wildlife, Albany, NY, USA

[27] Patricia Riexinger 2010. 2010-11 Official Guide to Laws and Regulations, New York Hunting and Trapping Vol. 4 Issue No. 1 Oct 2010. NYS Department of Environmental Conservation, Division of Fish, Wildlife & Marine, Albany, NY, USA.

CHAPTER III

BIOLOGICAL SURVEYS AND STUDIES

Game Protector Surveys

In 1940, the first New York Furbearer Project (W-1-R, Wildlife Research Job 1) was established and funded through the Pittman-Robertson Federal Aid in Wildlife Restoration Act. [1] At this time, beaver season decisions were based mainly on ground surveys conducted by game protectors and forest rangers. Part of the Furbearer Project's first responsibilities involved assisting the game protector force with analyzing and reporting their findings. Ground surveys in those early years estimated population size and changes in abundance from year to year by totaling all active colonies counted in the region and then multiplying by five. The average number of beavers in an active colony (five) originated from a Michigan study, which was then liberally extrapolated by staff wildlife biologists to annually provide tabulated estimates to the commissioner for consideration. [2] There was so much uncertainty regarding the accuracy of ground surveys, a better method of estimating the relative abundance of beavers was needed. However, the U.S. was shortly drawn into World War II, putting all research plans for wildlife in the state on indefinite hold.

Early Aerial Surveys

Following the war, the original Furbearer Project, relabeled (W-34-R, Wildlife Research Job 34)), began a study to determine the feasibility of using aerial surveys to estimate beaver abundance. Several returning biologists and former employees were Army Air Corps pilots who fought in WWII. They understood the importance of air planes for ground observation and their usefulness to wildlife surveys. Between 1946 and 1953, survey flights were conducted, at first over a portion of USGS quadrangles in a small area of the Adirondacks, and then on randomly selected flight lines. Parameters for successful observation, such as seasonable timing of flights, proper height above the ground, most appropriate speed and expected accuracy were all determined from this study. [3] A pilot and one observer were all that was needed. The employment of aerial observation following these early studies expanded beyond beaver to muskrat house counts, osprey and eagle nest counts, as well as other uses such as fish stocking in remote areas of the Adirondacks and lost people searches. To accommodate these new programs the Conservation Department formed a new office of aviation complete with their own planes and pilots. Two of the earliest veteran aviators employed by the Conservation Department were John Schemp and Steve Fordham. Together they amassed tens of thousands of flight hours in the 30 years they piloted Conservation Department planes. The lead and co-author in their early years with New York's Bureau of Wildlife both had the privilege of flying with these famous pioneer pilot/wildlife biologists before their retirement in the early 1980s.

In 1954 a series of randomly chosen aerial flight lines in the Adirondacks and eventually the Tug Hill Region were established and then employed to determine annual trends in beaver lodge counts well into the 1980's. (**Figure 4**) All lodges observed were counted within a narrow corridor along these lines, regardless of actual beaver activity. *"These strip aerial surveys provided inaccurate indices to populations because the effective search area could not be defined."* [4] Furthermore, beaver lodges remain intact and visible for several years after they have been abandoned, so little variation in the count between years was observed. This led to the perception that little usefulness for monitoring actual trends in beaver numbers could be found

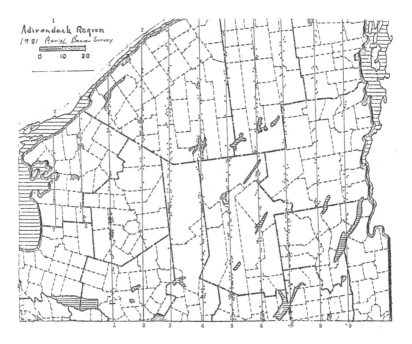

Figure 4. Early aerial survey used in the Adirondacks and Tug Hill from 1954-1980.

in conducting the surveys. Comments by Gary R. Parsons (Chief Wildlife Biologist, NYS Bureau of Wildlife) to the lead author, revealed this serious flaw in management application of early aerial surveys. *"As much as I hate to say it, management in the late 1960's wasn't paying any attention to these aerial surveys."* [5] Indeed, they were quickly abandoned in the early 1980s and replaced by random cluster sampling in most of New York.

Contemporary Aerial Surveys
The methodology for conducting aerial surveys actually began to change in the mid-1970s. In the southeastern Adirondacks, the co-author and Gary Parsons determined the reliability of aerial census for locating active beaver colonies over a specific and defined area, rather than north-south flight lines. [6] E. Michael Ermer in far western New York also initiated searches for active beaver colonies over a specific and defined area in the late 1970s. [7] Both studies proved one could

actually distinguish if a potential habitat site held an active beaver colony. Similar surveys in central and northwestern New York followed in the early 1980s. These newer survey methods used a random sample of whole 7.5-minute USGS Topographic maps covering specific wildlife management units. [8] Most of the seven upstate New York DEC Regions began using USGS quadrangle maps to survey the landscape for active beaver colonies by the mid-1980s.

The first use of the 1982 beaver survey in central New York involved an analysis of beaver activity on state reforestation areas. These lands showed only a slight difference in the occupation rate between private land in the same ecological zone (21.4% vs 20.7%, respectively). [9] The second use of these aerial survey data entailed a sample analysis of beaver activity on trout streams in central New York, requested by the Regional Fisheries Manager, Clifford Creech. In central New York any natural or man-made modification that causes further stream warming was seen by fisheries biologists as extremely detrimental to stream trout habitat. These same concerns had been expressed countless times by other fisheries biologists, since the first reintroduction of beavers into the Adirondack Mountains of New York early in the 20th century. The data revealed that 55 (16%) of the 344 active colonies discovered in the glaciated Appalachian Plateau of south-central NY DEC Region 7 were on trout streams. If beaver populations here were to be managed at a 30% occupation rate, the lead author projected another 28 (8%) more active beaver colonies on trout streams above the 55 already found in this area in 1982. [10] At the time the fisheries manager for central New York did not see this level of beaver occupation as detrimental to trout stream habitat in his region of responsibility. However, as beaver populations began to climb through the 1990s due to a shrinking number of trappers and the decline in world fur markets, he began to be more concerned about the future of stream trout habitat.

In the late 1980s, Joseph E. Lamendola (an original member of the NYS Beaver Management Team from the Watertown, NY wildlife office) suggested a major change to the random sample of whole USGS Quadrangles for beaver surveys. He proposed quartering the 7.5-minute quadrangle maps, centering a 2x3 mile rectangle in each quarter,

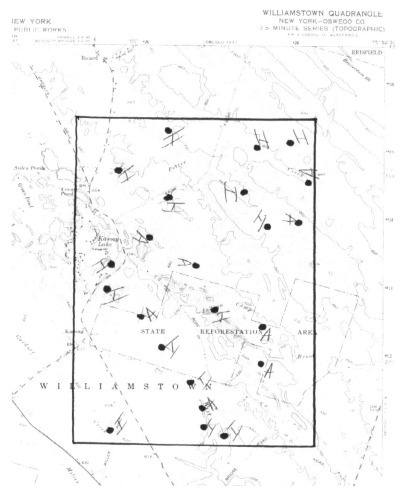

Figure 5. 2x3 mi. aerial survey plots became the statewide norm after 1992.
A = Active Colony Location I = Inactive Colony Location

labeling the quarters and then selecting a random sample of these survey rectangles for each wildlife management unit to be periodically
surveyed. (**Figure 5**) Potential habitat sites were then marked on these
sample plots and numbered for later record keeping. This survey
strategy was implemented for most of the important New York Wildlife Management Units in the early 1990s. [11] By the mid-1990s the
wildlife office in Watertown, NY switched from using USGS maps to

current air photos with the original 6 square mile plots drawn in. In the St. Lawrence Valley, he found the number of potential habitat sites on each plot to be so numerous, it became too daunting to navigate and observe beaver activity using just USGS maps.

Typically, beaver colony surveys commenced right after leaf fall and before snow covered the ice on beaver ponds. In the Adirondacks, leaf fall begins by mid-October, whereas in southern New York leaf fall is around the last week in October. Usually, the safest period for conducting aerial beaver surveys occurs within a two-week period following leaf fall. Survey flights involved flying up and down the drainages, and around the shoreline of ponds and lakes on the survey plots. Flying at close to stall speed at two hundred to five hundred feet above the ground was the usual practice. Stall refers to the aircraft wing's ability to generate lift. It does not mean the engine quits. The speed at which stall occurs varies greatly depending on several factors including air speed.

Wildlife observers recorded whether a potential site was active or inactive right on the survey maps, as the plane banked slightly over a site. Active sites observed in locations not already marked as potential sites on the maps became a new potential beaver colony location. For the most part, observers also acted as navigator, relieving the pilot of this distracting activity and keeping the survey on track. An active colony designation required at least three of the following seven features: fresh winter food cache, intact dam, freshly mudded dams, visible cuttings sometimes called *"shine"* by trappers, muddy water near dams, active trails on land and freshly flooded or stressed trees. [12] (**Figure 6**)

While aerial observation for beaver colonies and other wildlife and fisheries related purposes was a tremendous step forward in efficiency and accuracy, there were problems that the methodology highlighted. Many staff exhibited motion sickness even in normal, straight and level flight. This problem was exacerbated by the need for the pilots to make abrupt maneuvers such as tight circles, high angle banks and rapid ascent and decent to keep the objective in sight and enable staff to effectively observe the beaver lodges and dams. While over-the-counter or prescription medication could help prevent

Figure 6. Aerial survey of several active beaver ponds in 3 Rivers WMA, Baldwinsville, NY.

motion sickness, not all staff took it or it was ineffective. Many flights were terminated due to crew sickness.

Aerial reconnaissance of potential beaver habitats in central New York drew great interest from fisheries staff and Environmental Conservation officers. Low level flights over the varied terrain of central New York encouraged these groups to desire a place on the plane while Bureau of Wildlife staff conducted these surveys in the fall. On one such occasion the lead author invited a fisheries biologist to go along. He advised this biologist to take an over-the-counter medication for motion sickness two hours before the flight lifted off to ward off potential motion sickness. Upon arrival at the airport, this fisheries biologist showed up having disregarded the lead author's advice. According to him, if he could set nets in rolling seas on Lake Ontario, he could handle the high G forces of a plane tightly circling a beaver pond. From the time the plane left the air field to the time it reached the first sample plot in level flight, this particular biologist continu-

Figure 7. Adirondack float plane used for aerial beaver surveys in the Adirondacks.

ously yammered about his experience on rocking boats in high seas, as well as asking questions about where we would start. Once the plane made two tight circles over an active pond, his talking over the head phone ceased. The lead author glanced over the front seat, and all he saw was pale green and a look of nausea on the face of this fisheries biologist. Motion sickness had simply overcome this toughened sea dog.

In other regional wildlife offices, many staff members refused to be involved in these surveys because of an issue with motion sickness. One biologist in the southeastern Adirondacks got motion sickness on the take-off (float plane) from the starting location, a northern Adirondack Lake. His total time on the survey was 15 minutes. Finding individuals who would fly in float planes, fixed wing or a helicopter was undeniability an often-difficult task. (**Figure 7**) Nonetheless, aerial beaver surveys throughout New York were completed more or less for nearly 20 years.

Standards for Low Level Aerial Surveys

The danger of aerial observation was not limited to motion sickness. On November 1, 1990, the lead author was nearly killed in a crash of a two-seat Cessna 152 high-wing airplane while conducting formal aerial beaver pond surveys in the Appalachian Plateau of southcentral New York. [13] (**Figure 8**) A power-on stall occurred when the pilot misjudged the capability of this small plane to ascend rapidly over a wooded ridge at an already low altitude and slow air speed. Because of this mishap, standards for conducting low-level aerial surveys were adopted by the NY Bureau of Wildlife and implemented during the following fall survey period. High-wing planes with at least 150 horsepower became the new standard. To reduce weight, fuel tanks would no longer be topped off. Flights would be limited to no less than 200 feet above the ground. [14]

The danger of low-level and slow air speed aerial surveys was not the only threat the lead author faced. In November 2001, three months after the attacks of September 11th, the lead author conducting a beaver pond survey near the Nine Mile Nuclear Power Plant in Oswego

Plane Crash in Woods Injures Two

The pilot and a passenger were slightly injured when this Cessna airplane crashed Thursday in the woods near Sherburne, Chenango County Thursday. The plane was carrying a state biologist looking for signs of beaver activity.

By MIKE DICKINSON
The Post-Standard

SHERBURNE — A state wildlife observer looking for beavers was

Figure 8. The lead author nearly lost his life in 1990 while surveying beaver ponds in NY.

County, a fully armed Coast Guard helicopter radioed on the pilot's headset ordering our aircraft to cease and desist activities near this facility until he knew our intentions. After several tense minutes and conversations with air traffic control in Syracuse, NY, which confirmed our state sanctioned survey mission, the Coast Guard helicopter finally advised us to get no nearer the power plant and then broke off his intercept. Needless to say, it was just another frightening moment for pilot and observer while conducting a dangerous wildlife survey.

Potential Beaver Habitat

Prior to the 1970s, beaver population trends were monitored without any indication of how their abundance related to potentially available beaver habitat. In the late 1960s, a wildlife biologist assigned to the southern Adirondack district developed a method to better relate where beaver populations were relative to available beaver habitat. [15] Nathaniel Dickinson defined potential habitat sites as those locations with suitable topographic, edaphic (related to particular soil conditions, as a texture or drainage, rather than by physiographic or climate factors) and hydrologic characteristics that could be colonized by beaver, if suitable foods were available. This definition recognized the cyclic nature of beaver habitat use, where sites could be occupied by beaver for a time, abandoned, rejuvenated by plant succession and then re-occupied.

Dickinson concluded that evidence of beaver activity on recent air photos could be used to estimate the percentage of existing beaver activity on potential beaver habitat locations. He called this parameter occupation rate. The occupation rate could be used to measure how close beaver populations were to carrying capacity over a large geographic area. In northern New York where there is a long history of extensive beaver activity, his method worked extremely well. The coauthor and Gary Parsons were the first to apply Dickinson's technique for recognizing potential beaver habitat sites by interpretation of air photos on 964 square miles. [16] This technique in the remainder of New York, where beavers had been thoroughly suppressed for 30 years, required significant adaptation to merely using simple air photos a decade later.

Air photos in conjunction with USGS topographic maps and specific criteria based on topographic characteristics were found to be needed by E. Michael Ermer, a wildlife biologist assigned to western New York. [17] Meanwhile in south central New York a few years later, the lead author advanced a beaver habitat model similar in process to GAP Analysis. [18] It used overlays of the state's freshwater wetlands inventory, USGS topographic maps and vegetative and stream gradient criteria. Since New York had already produced wetland vegetation maps, and USGS topographic maps existed before WWII, this new approach provided a less expensive method for delineating potential beaver habitat and gave results comparable to both of the other earlier methods.

Experimental Trapping Season Closures

In the mid-1970s, the co-author and Gary Parsons, biologists in the southeastern Adirondacks, used Dickinson's method for identifying potential beaver colony locations. In addition, they used fall aerial surveys, rather than aerial photographs to determine the occupation rate of these sites. [19] Their evaluation showed the effects of closing trapping seasons on beaver occupation rates and clearly demonstrated that beaver populations could be suppressed by trapping.

Season closures were also evaluated in other parts of northern New York a short time later with similar results. [20] [21] Most importantly, these experiments with season manipulation proved beaver populations can be regulated by adjusting the timing and duration of the trapping season. [22] Management experience since then, for the most part, corroborated this conclusion. [23]

Several other studies conducted during the late 1970s and early 1980s examined such parameters as yearling reproduction, rates of harvest that stabilize populations and average maximum occupation rates beyond which habitat degradation occurs. [24] [25] The co-author and Gary Parsons studied population dynamics and rates of beaver occupancy in the mountainous, harsh terrain of the Adirondacks. These studies clearly articulated occupation rates between 30 and 40 percent, as biologically ideal for sustaining long term populations here. [26]

At first biologists were quick to use the number of potential habitat sites to calculate the occupation rate and from this estimate the total number of active colonies for a WMU. Indeed, it was seen as *"the most meaningful of all beaver objectives"* because it allows the manager to set a specific target and then develop a plan to achieve that target. [27] Both parameters were initially seen as critical for determining appropriate harvest targets and subsequent trapping seasons. However, in most of New York outside of the Adirondacks where beavers were uncommon, inaccurate estimates of potential habitat led to serious questions on the efficacy of using occupation rate for an objective. [28] Such a relative metric over time increased the actual population, as more potential beaver colony sites were discovered. In most of New York, potential beaver habitat was continually increasing as land use changed in the last quarter of the 20th century. Marginal farms, many on wet soils, steadily declined and revegetated with shrubs, like speckled alder, black willow, red osier dogwood and quaking aspen, favorite foods and building materials of beavers. A 30% occupation rate objective on 100 originally identified potential habitat sites in a WMU equated to 30 active colonies. Over time, as the number of potential habitat sites naturally increased through plant succession, a 30% occupation rate objective meant an actual rise in the number of active colonies.

Biologists working on beaver management throughout New York finally recognized that occupation rates only measured the relationship between the actual beaver population and the population objective. In the late 1990s, they embraced active beaver colonies/mi^2, as the absolute metric for estimating population size. This metric could be directly estimated from survey plot data and then compared to the occupation rate objective expressed as active colonies/mi^2. It was also seen as a more appropriate, accurate measure for estimating total active colonies in a wildlife management unit, associating this number to data on human tolerance to beaver damage and then directly applying these estimates to establish harvest quotas for next season. The ultimate goal of beaver management in the end was to achieve the right balance between the benefits and costs, both financial and societal, associated with beavers.

Wetland Values

Since the late 1940s, management of wetlands, as waterfowl habitat, has been and still is a major part of New York's wildlife program. The Federal Aid in Wildlife Restoration Project (W-48-D), begun in the late 1940s, had by 1958 built over 2,000 small marshes on public and private land to enhance waterfowl production throughout New York. Many of these small marshes were maintained by the NYS Bureau of Wildlife well into the 1970s. In addition, from the 1950s through the 1980s, thousands of acres of wetlands were acquired and developed into public Waterfowl Management Areas through Federal Aid in Wildlife Restoration Projects like W-20-R, W-32-R, W-36-R, W-47-R, W-52-R, W-61-R and W-94-R. [29] Little attention, however, was paid to quantifying waterfowl benefits produced from either small man-made marshes or beaver pond wetlands until the 1960s and 1970s. Apparently, the wildlife management philosophy at this time believed it was better to build and maintain small marshes, whose water level could be controlled, rather than managing for higher populations of natural pond builders, accompanied by issues of unwanted damage complaints.

Prior to New York several states in the Northeast, such as Maine in 1956 [30] [31], Massachusetts in 1965 [32] and New Hampshire in 1968 [33], examined waterfowl use and production in beaver ponds to clarify the importance of actively managing beavers in their respective waterfowl management programs. Other states in the Southeast [34] [35], and even in the mountainous West [36] studied the relationship between waterfowl and beavers much before New York. It took nearly a decade after other states had already begun studies of beavers and waterfowl before New York finally initiated formal studies of their own.

Documentation of duckling production on active and inactive beaver ponds in the southeastern Adirondacks attested to their value as waterfowl habitats. On a survey of 28 beaver ponds (700 acres in total), .115 broods per acre was observed. On 13 small man-made marshes constructed in the same area under the W-48-D Project, 118 acres produced a mere .035 broods per acre. A comparison of maintenance costs and duck broods per acre confirmed that maintenance costs on these small marshes were 24 times more than the cost of handling beaver complaints in the same geographic area. The fact that beaver ponds also produced three times as many duck broods compared to man-made small marshes unmistakably demonstrated that beavers and their pond building activities were more effective constructing small marshes for waterfowl than building and maintaining small marshes under the W-48-D Federal Aid Project. [37]

In far western New York, beaver related wetland benefits clearly substantiated a better cost/benefit ratio for increasing beaver populations to create small marshes, than traditional small marsh construction and maintenance, even with a highly service-oriented beaver complaint response. [38] In the mid-1980s several regional wildlife offices embarked on a policy of increasing the beaver population in most of the state historically held well below the ideal population level for long term sustainability. At this time the average estimated size of beaver impoundments in New York was about 15 acres. [39] [40] [41] By increasing the number of active beaver colonies from 3,200 in 1975 to a goal of approximately 14,000 in 1990, a conservative estimate of about 210,000 acres of shallow water wetland impoundments would be produced annually by beavers. [42] (**Figure 9**) This was 162,000 acres more than the 48,000 acres created by beavers in the 1970s. At the time few states, if any, were using beaver pond building activity to enhance wetland benefits. An article in *Outdoor Life Magazine* in 1991 revealed that the NY DEC won national recognition from the US Fish & Wildlife Service for its innovative beaver management program which balanced wetland habitat benefits with the public costs of handling beaver-human conflict. [43]

Using duckling production data (.75 ducks/acre) from the southern Adirondacks, New York beaver colonies conservatively produced about 157,000 ducks in 1990. [44] Waterfowl Surveys in the St. Lawrence River Valley in the spring of 1994 further demonstrated the value of beaver impoundments to duck production. Bryan Swift (NY Bureau of Wildlife Waterfowl Specialist) in a letter to the president of

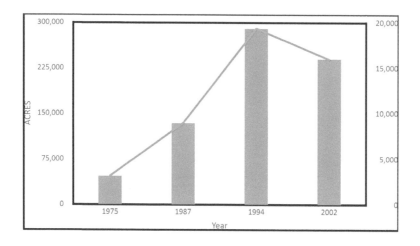

Figure 9. Acreage of beaver impoundments over time in New York.
Average Acreage of a NY beaver impoundment = 15 acres: After Gotie 1988, Ermer 1990, Lamendola 1990 Number Active colonies in NY: 1975 - Bishop et.al. 1992. 1987 – Gotie et.al. 1988.
1994 – Batcheller 1992. 2002 – Gotie et.al. 2004.

Northern Ecological Associates, Inc. wrote, *"Breeding pair densities of all duck species were much higher on survey plots with beaver ponds during both survey visits."* [45] Significant annual increases between 1989 and 1999 in Atlantic Flyway spring breeding surveys for wood duck, mallard and black duck pairs suggested that substantial increases in active beaver ponds during these years played a major role in waterfowl production in this flyway. [46] Unfortunately, comparison of spring nesting pair counts in wetlands impounded by beaver dams in New York has never been systematically examined on a statewide basis over the 25 plus years of conducting this federally sanctioned waterfowl survey. [47]

Implementation of the North American Waterfowl Management Plan in New York signified one giant forward step toward recognizing the true value of beaver shaped wetlands in waterfowl production. [48] Much of this plan focused on the St. Lawrence Valley, because the number of active beaver colonies impounded approximately 39,000 acres of land in 1994. This level of beaver activity, however, vastly exceeded the population objective for this area. [49] It nearly cost the NYS Department of Environmental Conservation the authority to manage beavers here for any legitimate reason, due to the loss of public trust in New York's ability to manage this important mammal. Providing sufficient funding for gaining greater public support for beavers seemed necessary. [50]

Waterfowl were not the only group of wildlife to benefit from an increase in beaver created wetlands. In the late 1990s and early 2000s studies conducted on the herpetological fauna also bore further witness to the existence value active beaver ponds and beaver modified wetlands provided for New York's less studied vertebrate fauna. Of New York's 61 reptiles and amphibians, not including the sea turtles in New York, beaver ponds provided habitats for 34% of these lesser appreciated wildlife species. [51] It is now generally recognized that beavers are important managing agents of wetlands and their impoundments are also highly beneficial to a variety of birds, mammals, reptiles and amphibians. [52] [53] Few if any states or provinces managed beaver with this in mind in the 1960s and 1970s. Few do so today.

Trap Studies

In 1949 the Conservation Department fixed the beaver and otter seasons to coincide. [54] This action set in motion a future issue with combining two distinct and completely different fur-bearing mammal species into one harvest management strategy, that has persisted in most of New York for the last 70 years. For the most part, beaver and otter share similar habitats. The harvest management programs of New York for both species has always involved trappers taking both in the same trap set locations and with the same types of traps. It was because of these factors that the Conservation Department initially linked the trapping seasons of both species together.

In the last decade of the 20th century, a public/state project designed to return the river otter to the aquatic environments of central and western New York, where they had been absent for more than

Figure 10. A major research undertaking with #330™ beaver trap was concluded in 2002.

150 years, set off a conflict with a specific type of beaver trap commonly used for trapping both species throughout New York. A mail survey of trappers conducted in 1996 demonstrated that the rotating jaw of a 10"x10" Conibear #330™ trap commonly deployed and efficiently used for beaver trapping, overlapped the catch rate efficiency and proportion of trap set locations used to catch otter. [55] The NY Bureau of Wildlife concluded that improvement in river otter management was contingent on finding a more selective beaver trap. [56]

New York's Conservation Commission/Department long ago recognized the importance of beaver trapping to the long-term health of beaver populations in the state. However, because the traps and sets used to regulate beaver populations clearly posed a significant conflict with river otter population management in central and western New York, the NY Furbearer Management Team (FMT) in 1998, initiated a two-stage study of trigger designs that would allow greater capture selectivity with the # 330™ trap. [57] (**Figure 10**) A more selective beaver trap, they reasoned, would allow New York to separate the harvest of beaver from otter and improve population management for both species.

The first phase of study involved a controlled experiment in a specially modified fish hatchery raceway at Hale Creek Station with captive beaver and otter. Conclusions revealed the Top Side Parallel trigger (TSP) by far met the objective of a high firing rate on beavers and a low firing rate on otters. Phase two was conducted on actual trap lines throughout New York employing pairs of TSP triggers and commonly employed Standard V trigger configured traps. These field studies showed an identical beaver catch rate between these two significantly different trigger configurations. Further field study in North Carolina resulted in a 50% reduction in otter catch rate with the TSP trigger compared to the otter catch rate with the Standard V. This work provided evidence that a simple modification of the standard trigger on the #330 trap could make this trap effective for beavers and more selective against capturing river otter. In 2005 New York imposed a new trigger regulation where otters were completely protected following this study.[58]

Pelt Values

Throughout the history of beaver management in NY, seasonal trapping harvest over large sections of the NY landscape has been the method of choice for checking the growth of beaver populations. Yet, before 1980 little information was systematically collected on the value of pelts brought to fur markets in NY. It has been our experience that most trappers during the 20th century sold their beaver pelts to local fur buyers or fur auctions hosted by county trapper's associations. (**Figure 11**) Since then, more trappers now directly ship their pelts to the large international auctions, like the Fur Harvesters Auction, Inc. of North Bay, Ontario or North American Fur Auctions, Inc. of Toronto, Ontario, where presumably they receive a higher average price.

As global demand for furs expanded during the 1970s, there grew more interest by New York biologists in furbearer harvest management in the state. Over-harvest and rapid declines in furbearer pop-

Figure 11. County fur auction - Independent Fur Harvesters of Central NY –
1980s.

ulations due to significant increases in pelt values over earlier years
concerned the biologists of New York. It led them to acquire annual
average pelt values for all thirteen species of mammals classified as
furbearers. Between the 1979-80 and 2004-05 trapping seasons, fur
auction records from Maine to Pennsylvania were obtained from
published results enumerated in the *Trapper and Predator Caller
Magazine*. Additionally, summaries were sent directly to the lead author from fur auctions held by New York county trapper associations. Pelt values by species were then combined into a composite
average for that season. **(Figure 12)**

Armed with this information along with extrapolated estimates
of harvest assembled from New York's pelt sealing reports and surveys of trappers and fur hunters, the NY Bureau of Wildlife was finally able to annually calculate the total value of New York's raw fur
production. (**Table 2.**) This data helped furbearer biologists better
understand the economic importance of the fur market and how it
could affect trapper participation and subsequent harvest on furbearer populations.

The ultimate use of annual pelt value estimates over time was to

Season	Muskrat	Mink	Beaver	R.Otter	Raccoon	Bobcat	Coyote
1979-80	$6,089,480	$401,100	$570,370	$42,008	$11,394,750	$21,001	$45,808
1980-81	$4,026,888	$325,025	$293,582	$35,797	$8,061,740	$19,729	$36,492
1981-82	$2,189,254	$305,999	$119,391	$14,083	$11,049,805	$16,000	$1,705,775
1982-83	$1,808,329	$257,020	$150,090	$18,111	$6,794,135	$13,826	$56,998
1983-84	$1,282,204	$224,264	$138,563	$18,029	$4,237,966	$10,268	$28,303
1984-85	$1,314,965	$268,151	$232,182	$17,305	$7,330,568	$12,359	$45,445
1985-86	$874,482	$272,243	$343,997	$14,599	$6,131,113	$12,263	$25,286
1986-87	$1,383,924	$367,087	$594,737	$27,190	$7,244,154	$18,558	$30,401
1987-88	$1,714,076	$452,621	$441,781	$30,069	$4,818,862	$16,424	$24,8650
1988-89	$489,923	$379,874	$249,922	$17,445	$1,464,498	$8,535	$15,848
1989-90	$120,218	$178,993	$276,006	$20,768	$560,809	$4,703	$9,341
1990-91	$141,706	$153,424	$122,696	$10,848	$378,003	$1,036	$8,099
1991-92	$296,934	$277,634	$177,880	$21,263	$1,292,164	NDA	$29,126
1992-93	$219,553	$186,840	$133,824	$32,681	$962,633	$4,594	$23,940
1993-94	$316,988	$137,738	$345,486	$65,781	$1,221,623	$8,733	$32,354
1994-95	$505,341	$130,821	$568,768	$99,254	$1,065,091	$8,719	$38,036
1995-96	$297,814	$101,339	$435,842	$32,716	$922,189	$7,673	$30,431
1996-97	$977,958	$276,407	$749,922	$73,813	$2,829,769	$7,446	$51,471
1997-98	$640,854	$193,536	$472,401	$43,843	$991,627	$11,471	$33,628

Table 2. Estimated Value of Wild Fur Harvested in New York (1980 – 1998) [1]

[1] *Robert F. Gotie 1998. Fur Harvest Statistics – Update (1980 – 1998). Memo (October 1, 1998) to NY Bureau of Wildlife Furbearer Information Group. Cortland, NY, USA.*
Note: Between 1980 and 1998 Furbearer harvest estimates were collected by a statistically reliable telephone Survey of Trappers and Furbearer Hunters. After 1998 these same statistics were estimated by using a less reliable mail survey

Red Fox	Gray Fox	Opossum	Skunk	Marten	Fisher	Weasel	Total Value
$2,536,275	$1,425,796	$153,00	$60,750	NDA	$280,345	NDA	$23,020,684
$1,744,555	$920,976	$98,100	$50,850	NDA	$125,434	NDA	$15,739,166
$1,705,775	$842,159	$85,526	$38,667	NDA	$93,309	NDA	$16,522,000
$1,404,638	$761,948	$80,372	$47,222	NDA	$59,064	NDA	$11,451,753
$867,386	$735,155	$66,199	$23,799	NDA	NDA	NDA	$7,632,137
$1,089,877	$610,652	$89,862	$17.324	NDA	NDA	NDA	$11,028,690
$636,180	$449,798	$88,365	$19,299	NDA	$166,884	NDA	$9,054,509
$874,992	$516,912	$90,637	$13,610	NDA	$134,998	NDA	$11,297,200
$526,995	$558,6070	$88,881	$18,707	NDA	$207,091	NDA	$8,898,963
$369,679	$212,170	$29,793	$14,210	NDA	$56,734	NDA	$3,308,631
$141,936	$66,914	$10,009	$2,044	$330	$28,040	NDA	$1,420,110
$92,344	$29,920	$9,335	$6,165	$500	$13,353	NDA	$970,428
$229,111	$165,032	$14,953	$5,010	NDA	$12,252	NDA	$2,529,745
$141,005	$48,777	$10,057	$6,008	$873	$12,252	NDA	$1,783,038
$145,547	$53,157	$7,282	$4,367	$852	$17,517	$483	$2,357,910
$247,065	$55,286	$8,607	$7,456	NDA	$19,582	NDA	$2,754,028
$278,033	$97,730	$10,287	$11,457	NDA	$26,091	NDA	$2,251,602
$505,064	$203,868	$21,964	$19,321	NDA	$52,944	NDA	$5,769,947
$207,708	$117,496	$18,770	$14,751	$3,752	$63,843	NDA	$2,809,927

conducted by Cornell Univ., Human Dimensions Research Unit.
As such, the NY Bureau of Wildlife ceased estimating the economic value of furbearers harvested in NY.

	AVERAGE		TOTAL
SPECIES	$ VALUE per PELT**	TOTAL HARVEST***	$ VALUE OF NY FURS
MUSKRAT	$2.92		NDA
MINK	$9.91		NDA
BEAVER	$18.15		$0
OTTER	$47.93		$0
RACCOON	$7.91		NDA
BOBCAT	ERR		ERR
COYOTE	$14.54		$0
RED FOX	$16.10		NDA
GRAY FOX	$8.78		NDA
OPOSSUM	$1.52		NDA
SKUNK	$3.05		NDA
MARTEN	$21.38		$0
FISHER	$17.55		$0
WEASEL	$3.50		NDA
TOTAL			ERR

ESTIMATED VALUE OF RAW FURS PRODUCED IN NEW YORK FOR THE 2000-01 HUNTING AND TRAPPING SEASON Dec, Jan, Feb, 7 NY, 6 PA, 1 VT, 1 CT, 1NH AS OF 3/20/2001

** SOURCE: THE TRAPPER AND PREDATOR CALLER, SPEARMAN PUBLISHING AND PRINTING, INC, REGULAR FEATURE - ASSOCIATION NEWS: NY, PA, NH, VT, CT,
*** 1999-00 PELT SEAL REPORT
NDA = NO DATA AVAILABLE AT THIS DATE ON HARVEST

Figure 12. Composite average of pelt values from the Northeastern US Trapper Auctions.

develop a model for predicting the harvest of beavers given prevailing pelt values and gasoline costs. The cost to travel from one's home base to one's trapping grounds, especially for gasoline, has long been considered relevant to trapper participation in New York. However, it has never been fully examined by New York biologists. The lead author and Michael Runge (doctoral candidate, Cornell Univ.) collaborated to design this model, which could improve the setting of annual harvest quotas directly useful for establishing appropriate trapping seasons. [59] It was last used in central NY for the 2004-05 fall to spring trapping season.

Decline in the Value of Wild Furs

Supply and demand, along with the shrinking value of the US dollar, play a pivotal role in the market value of commodities. [60] Taken together these factors combined to reduce the overall value of beaver pelts in New York through the 20th century. (**Figure 13**) Population declines of other once abundant furbearers, like muskrats and racoons, [61] dynamic changes in all other harvested furbearer populations, as well as the move by New Yorkers away from fur fashion, have together with declining pelt values further reduced interest in fur trapping through the later years of the 20th century. (**Table 3**) If these

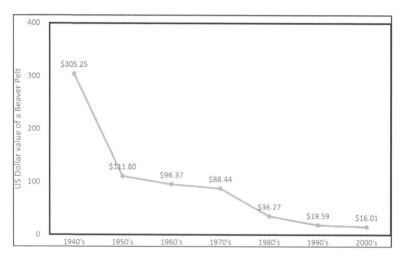

Figure 13. The purchasing value of a beaver pelt between the 1940s and 2000s.

1940s Value: Adirondack Record-Elizabethtown Post 4/6/1944, $70 for XXXL pelt reported

Average value extrapolated from difference between XXXL and XL-Genesee Valley Trappers Auctions 2012

1950s, '60s, '70s from Henry Hilton 1986.Beaver Assessment. Maine Dept. Inland Fisheries and Wildlife, Bangor ME, USA.

1980's, '90's, 2000's from Robert F. Gotie 2005. Unpublished data, NY Bureau of Wildlife, Region 7, Cortland, NY Pelt Value received by Trappers adjusted by the value of a dollar (base year 2005) reported in mykindred.com.

trends continue well into the 21st century, we may all be witness to the demise of fur trapping in New York, similar to California's ban on fur trapping. [62] If fur trapping is no longer acceptable, it will need to be replaced by damage control trappers who will charge a fee for their pest removal service, or return to government agents depopulating vast areas of the state where beavers create conflict with people, agriculture and infrastructure. In any event the management of beaver populations for the many benefits they provide will be lost.

Trappers

Licensed trappers, especially those who target beaver, have been an integral partner in furbearer management in New York since 1924. Nationwide, sportsmen (hunters and trappers) have supported wildlife programs through license fees and taxes on ammunition and firearms for nearly a century through the Federal Pittman-Robertson and Dingle-Johnson programs. Moreover, these monies deposited into New York's Conservation Fund have supported numerous wildlife programs over the decades.

One of the most important cooperative efforts in 1980 included the development and implementation of a mandatory trapper training course for first time trappers in New York. Trappers participate by teaching the courses, reviewing content for improvements and revision of the trapper training manual. *Trapping Responsibly in the 1990s, New York's Advanced Trapper Training Seminars and Trapping in the 21st Century* have all been educational programs for trappers by trappers initiated in New York during the 20th century. Without trapper participation, the development of Best Management Practices (BMPs) for trapping in the US and Canada, including the BMP for beaver trapping, would not have been possible.

In so far as beavers are concerned, New York trappers have been directly involved in numerous beaver research studies, such as those conducted in Fulton, Warren, Washington and in the Moose River area of Hamilton County, to name a few. Trappers have also voluntarily cooperated in studies of fisher, marten, coyotes, otter, bobcat and mink by supplying fresh specimens utilized for biological analysis of population age and sex, food habits, reproduction, body weight,

Table 3. Trapping License Sales in New York 1940 – 2003

Year	License Sales	Year	License Sales	Year	License Sales	Year	License Sales
1940	8,403	1960	8,526	1980	32,520	2000	8,412
1941	17,802	1961	7,877	1981	27,972	2001	8,044
1942	17,243	1962	8,065	1982	25,491	2002	10,640
1943	12,034	1963	8,835	1983	20,000	2003	10,142
1944	16,104	1964	8,349	1984	19,259	2004	NDA
1945	11,995	1965	8,650	1985	16,552	2005	NDA
1946	22,535	1966	8,241	1986	17,290	2006	NDA
1947	17,249	1967	6,764	1987	18,713	2007	NDA
1948	20,167	1968	8,342	1988	16,050	2008	NDA
1949	19,369	1969	9,539	1989	12,514	2009	NDA
1950	14,729	1970	8,884	1990	9,671	2010	NDA
1951	15,174	1971	9,076	1991	8,212	2011	NDA
1952	17,043	1972	11,725	1992	7,559	2012	NDA
1953	15,997	1973	15,437	1993	6,958	2013	NDA
1954	12,349	1974	16,827	1994	7,967	2014	NDA
1955	12,771	1975	15,504	1995	7,783	2015	NDA
1956	12,170	1976	17,545	1996	7,446	2016	NDA
1957	10,969	1977	19,483	1997	9,055	2017	NDA
1958	8,804	1978	22,527	1998	9,405	2018	NDA
1959	9,152	1979	31,504	1999	9,632	2019	NDA

Total Licenses sold includes Resident, Non-Resident and Junior Trapping Licenses. The Junior Trapping License requirement for Trappers under age 16 began in the 1980-81 Season.
Information on License Sales obtained from the following sources:
Kathy Loconti-Lee 1993. NY Trapping License Sales. Memo to NY DEC Regional Wildlife Managers, May 25, 1993
NY Bureau of Wildlife Fur Project, Albany, NY, USA.
Frank S. Phillips 1989. Table of NY Trapping License Sales from 1940 through license years 1989, July 1989, NY Bureau of Wildlife,
Fur Project, Albany, NY, USA.
Anonymous 1993. License Sales for 1979 through 2003 provided by NYS DEC Revenue Accounting Unit, May 1993, Albany, NY, USA.

inorganic bio-toxins and species development and evolution. [63] [64] [65] Besides legally harvested fresh furbearer specimens, licensed trappers have provided information on their trapping activities such as trap nights, trap types, type of sets, and set locations through diaries and formal surveys. They have earnestly reported information on their harvests and trapping activity for decades through the volunteer trapper telephone and mail surveys conducted throughout the state. Information collected over the years through these surveys delivered important insight directly used for improving management actions in the later years of the 20th century.

States like Vermont and Pennsylvania benefited by New York trappers cooperating in capturing live furbearers to help these states re-establish viable pine marten and fisher populations during the 1990s. [66] [67] Without New York trappers, a sustaining fisher population in the Catskills and a viable population of river otters in central and western New York would be unheard of today. [68] It is without a doubt that experienced and licensed trappers from New York played the pivotal role in the success of these trap and transfer programs in New York and elsewhere.

New York landowners and highway departments have annually experienced hundreds of beaver-human conflicts during the 1990s, as populations of this problematic mammal grew over time. Many of these issues were resolved by licensed trappers who provided their trapping skills in removing problem beavers during the open beaver trapping season. Furthermore, many of these same New York trappers became licensed animal control agents to help people overcome their wildlife conflict after trapping seasons close. Through legal trapping seasons and permitted removal by licensed trappers of problem beavers, populations of this species have, for the most part, been managed to acceptable levels throughout New York, helping to further reduce the occurrence of density dependent transmissible diseases, like tularemia, beaver fever, rabies and canine distemper.

Working with trappers, their county associations and the NY Trapper Organization was at times rewarding and sometimes intimidating. Trapper associations were usually led by the most veteran trappers, and they generally knew more about furbearing mammal behavior than most wildlife biologists including the two authors of this narrative.

Sometimes a lone trapper comes along that is more hilarious than intimidating. One such trapper would come to the Cortland wildlife office often looking to get his beaver pelts sealed. You knew he was about by the smell of skunk wafting through the hallway. Always he would be wearing hip-boots, a raggedy old wool shirt and a small caliber pistol on his hip. On one such occasion he brought in a dozen beaver pelts to be sealed. Instead of open skinning these pelts, as is customary, he had skinned them cased, like you would do with muskrats. Why he did this is anyone's guess. But certainly, it was a foolhardy move on his part, rendering the value of these pelts to nearly nothing. Of course, most trappers we both knew over the course of our careers were not only knowledgeable, but smart enough to know how to finish a pelt for the maximum economic value. Beaver trapping was by far the most labor-intensive activity in the fur trade.

Over the course of furbearer conservation management in New York during the 20th century, we cannot overstate the importance of trappers and the role they played as valued participants. The amount of taxes and Conservation Fund money they saved the NY Division of Fish & Wildlife alone with their knowledge and dedication to the craft of trapping merits by itself our thanks and gratitude.

References

[1] 30th Annual Report of the Conservation Department New York, 1940.

[2] G. W. Bradt 1938. A Study of Beaver Colonies in Michigan. Journal of Mammalogy 19: 139-162.

[3] Arthur H. Cook. 1954. Determination of Trends in Abundance of Beavers – Develop Methods of Survey to Determine Trends in Beaver Populations. NYS Conservation Department, Federal Aid in Wildlife Restoration, Final Report W-80-R-1, Albany, NY, USA.

[4] Paul G. Bishop, Mark K. Brown, Russel. Cole, E. Michael Ermer, Robert F. Gotie, Joseph E. Lamendola, Bruce Penrod, Scott Smith and William Sharick 1992. Beaver Management in New York State: History and Specification of Future Program. NYS Department of Environmental

Conservation, Publication, pp 12, Albany, NY, USA.

[5] Gary R. Parsons, 1988, Chief Wildlife Biologist, NYS DEC, 1988, Marginal Notes in Progress in Beaver Management.

[6] Mark K. Brown and Gary R. Parsons 1982. Reliability of Fall Aerial Censuses for Locating Active Beaver Colonies in Northern New York. NY Fish & Game Journal 29 (2)204-2.

[7] E. Michael Ermer 1980. Beaver Management Studies in Region 9. NYS Department of Environmental Conservation, Fed. Aid in Wildlife Restoration, unpublished Final Report Job 107, Project W-139-D, Olean, NY, USA.

[8] Robert F. Gotie 1982. Aerial Beaver Surveys in Central NY. NYS Department of Environmental Conservation, Bureau of Wildlife, Region 7, Fed. Aid in Wildlife Restoration, Special Report, Project W-137-D, Cortland, NY, USA.

[9] Robert F. Gotie 1983. Potential Beaver Habitat and Occupancy Rates for State Reforestation Lands in Region 7. Memo to J.C. Proud, Regional Wildlife Manager, NYS Bureau of Wildlife, Cortland, NY, USA.

[10] Robert F. Gotie 1983. Incidence of Beaver Colony Sites on Trout Waters in Region 7. Memo to J.C. Proud, Regional Wildlife Manager, NYS Bureau of Wildlife, Cortland, NY, USA.

[11] Paul G. Bishop et.al. 1992. op. cit.

[12] Paul G. Bishop et.al. 1992. op. cit.

[13] Mike Dickinson 1990. Plane Crash in Woods Injures Two. Syracuse Post Standard, November 2, 1990, Syracuse, NY.

[14] Paul G. Bishop et.al. 1992. op. cit.

[15] Nathanial R. Dickinson 1971. Aerial Photographs as an Aid in Beaver Management. NY Fish & Game Journal 18 (1):57-61.

[16] Mark k. Brown and Gary R. Parsons 1982. op. cit.

[17] E. Michael Ermer 1980. op. cit.

[18] Robert F. Gotie and Daryl L. Jenks 1984. Assessment of the Use of Wetland Inventory Maps for Determining Potential Beaver Habitat. NY Fish & Game Journal 31 (1): 55-62.

[19] Gary R. Parsons and Mark K. Brown 1978. An Assessment of Aerial Photographic Interpretation for Recognizing Potential Beaver Colony Sites. NY Fish & Game Journal 25 (2):175-177.

[20] Gary R. Parsons 1975. Effect of a Four-Year Closure of Trapping Season

for Beaver in Eastern Warren County. NY Fish and Game Journal 22 (1):57-61.

[21] Gary R. Parsons and Mark K. Brown 1978. Effects of a Four-Year Closure of a Trapping Season for Beaver in Fulton County. NY Fish & Game Journal 25 (1):23-30.

[22] Gary R. Parsons and Mark K. Brown 1981. Season Length as a Method of Achieving Population Objectives for Beaver (Castor Canadensis). World-wide Furbearer Conference Proceedings, pp 1392-1403.

[23] John F. Organ, Robert F. Gotie, Thomas A. Decker and Gordon R. Batcheller. 1996. A Case Study in the Sustained Use of Wildlife – The Management of Beaver in the Northeastern United States. SUI Technical Series Vol. 1:125-138, IUCN.

[24] Mark K. Brown 1980. Sex and Age Compositions and Reproductive Rates for Beaver Harvested During the Spring Trapping Seasons in Clinton, Franklin and Essex Counties – 1973 to 1976. NYS Department of Environmental Conservation, Fed. Aid in Wildlife Restoration, unpublished Final Report, Project W-135-D, Warrensburg, NY, USA.

[25] Mark K. Brown 1984. Moose River Beaver Harvest Study. NYS Department of Environmental Conservation, Fed. Aid in Wildlife Restoration, unpublished Final Report, Project W-135-D, Warrensburg, NY USA.

[26] Mark K. Brown 1983. The Results of 10 Consecutive Years of Trapping Seasons for Beaver in Fulton, County 1972-1983. NYS Department of Environmental Conservation, Fed Aid in Wildlife Restoration, unpublished Final Report, Project W-135-D, Warrensburg, NY, USA.

[27] Gary R. Parsons 1975. 1975-76 Program Year. Memo to Chief Wildlife Biologist from Regional Wildlife Manager, Project W-135S-D, NY DEC Region 5S Warrensburg, NY, USA.

[28] Robert F. Gotie 1998. Addendum to Beaver Management in New York 1992. For NYS Bureau of Wildlife, Statewide Furbearer Management Team Report – Central NY Staff Memo, NYS Department of Environmental Conservation, Cortland, NY, USA.

[29] Paul G. Bishop et.al. 1992. op. cit.

[30] Henry Hilton 1956. Waterfowl-Beaver Relations Study. Job Completion Report, Fed. Aid in Wildlife Restoration, Project w-37-R 5&6, Augusta, ME, USA.

[31] R.W. 1967. Management of Beaver to Benefit Waterfowl in Maine. Trans.

Northeast Fish and Wildlife Conference. 24:46-51.

[32] P.B. Stanton 1965. An Evaluation of Waterfowl Utilization on three Age Classes of Beaver Impoundments with Emphasis on the Black Duck.MS thesis, Univ. Massachusetts, Amherst, MA, USA.

[33] H.P. Nevers 1968. Waterfowl Utilization of Beaver impoundments in Southeastern New Hampshire. Scientific Contribution No. 431. Department of Forest Resources, University of New Hampshire, Durham, NH, USA.

[34] G.R. Hepp and J.D.Hair 1977. Wood Duck Brood Mobility and Utilization of Beaver Pond Habitats. Proc. Annual Conference Southeast Association of Fish and Wildlife Agencies. 31:216-225.

[35] D.H. Arner 1963. Production of Duck Food in Beaver Ponds. J. Wildlife Management. 27(1):76-81.

[36] L.G. 1955. A Study of Beaver-Waterfowl Relations in a Mountainous Area of Beaverhead County, Montana. MS thesis Montana State Univ., Missoula, MT, USA.

[37] Mark K. Brown and Gary R. Parsons 1979. Waterfowl Production on Beaver Flowages in a Part of Northern New York. NY Fish & Game Journal 26 (2): 142-153.

[38] E. Michael Ermer 1984. Analysis of Benefits and Management Costs Associated with Beaver in Western New York. NY Fish & Game Journal 31 (2): 119-132.

[39] Robert F. Gotie 1988. Area of Beaver Impoundments in Central New York. NYS Department of Environmental Conservation, Fed. Aid in Wildlife Restoration, unpublished Final Report, Project W-137-D, Cortland, NY, USA.

[40] E. Michael Ermer 1990. Unpublished Data, NYS Department of Environmental Conservation, Fed. Aid in Wildlife Restoration, Project W-139-D, Olean, NY, USA.

[41] Joseph E. Lamendola 1990. Unpublished Data. NYS, Department of Environmental Conservation, Fed. Aid in Wildlife Restoration, Project W-136-D, Watertown, NY, USA.

[42] Paul G. Bishop et.al. 1992. op. cit.

[43] Robert F. Gotie 1991. NY Receives Award for Beaver/Waterfowl Management, First State Wetland Conservation Award from US Fish & Wildlife Service. April Issue, Outdoor Life Magazine. Memo to Gary R. Parsons,

Chief Wildlife Biologist, Region 7 Cortland, NY, USA, July 19, 1991.

[44] Paul G. Bishop et.al. 1992. op. cit.

[45] Bryan Swift 1994. Results of Waterfowl Surveys in the St. Lawrence River Valley. Letter to David J. Santillo, Pres. Northern Ecological Associates, Inc. NY DEC Waterfowl Project, Albany, NY, USA.

[46] John T. Major 2003. Response to Complaint Letter about Length of Waterfowl Season and Liberal Bag Limits. NYS Bureau of Wildlife, Chief Wildlife Biologist, Letter to MS Rhonda Roaring, Albany, NY, USA.

[47] Thomas Bell 2018. Personal Communication. Sr. Wildlife Biologist NYS DEC, Region 7, Bureau of Wildlife, Cortland, NY, USA.

[48] Joseph E. Lamendola 1990. Support for Beaver Management in The St. Lawrence Valley Focus Area. Letter to Kenneth F. Wich - Director Division of Fish and Wildlife, NYS Department of Environmental Conservation, Region 6, Watertown, NY, USA.

[49] Paul G. Bishop 1990. Support for Beaver Management Funding. Letter to Joseph E. Lamendola Statewide Chairman – St. Lawrence Valley Focus Area, Acting Fur Project Leader, NYS Bureau of Wildlife, Albany, NY, USA.

[50] Paul G. Bishop 1990. op. cit.

[51] James P. Gibbs, Alvin R. Breisch, Peter K. Ducey, Glenn Johnson, John L. Behler and Richard G. Bothner 2007. The Amphibians and Reptiles of New York State: Identification, Natural History and Conservation. Oxford University Press.

[52] Anita M. Grover 1993. Influence of Beaver on Bird and Mammal Species Richness within Wetlands of Different Sizes in South-Central New York. MS Thesis, State University of New York, College of Environmental Sciences and Forestry, Syracuse, NY, USA.

[53] Anita M. Grover and Guy K. Baldassarre 1995. Bird Species Richness within Beaver Ponds in South-Central New York. Wetlands 15(2):108-118.

[54] Arthur Holweg 1949. Furbearer Seasons by Department Order. NYS Conservation Department, 39th Annual Report to the Legislature, Albany, NY, USA.

[55] Marie Kautz 1997. 1996 Trapper Mail Survey Report. NYS Department of Environmental Conservation, Fed Aid in Wildlife Restoration, Supplemental Report, Grant NY: W-173-G, Albany, NY, USA.

[56] Robert F. Gotie, Marie A. Kautz, Mark K. Brown and J. Edward Kautz 2000. Selectivity with #330™ Conibears. The Trapper and Predator

Caller Magazine. October 2000.

[57] Robert F. Gotie, J. Edward Kautz, Perry W. Sumner, Marie A. Kautz, Mark K. Brown and Jon Heisterberg 2005. A Modified Trigger for the 10"x10" Rotating Jaw Body Gripping Trap (#330 Coniber ™) for Selectively Taking Beaver. NYS Department of Environmental Conservation, Fed Aid in Wildlife Restoration, unpublished Final Report, Project W-173-G, Albany, NY, USA.

[58] John Major 2005. Hunting and Trapping Regulations Guide 2005-2006. NYS Department of Environmental Conservation. Publication, 39pp.

[59] Michael C. Runge, Robert F. Gotie, D.H. Streeter and Aaron N. Moen 1998. A Time Series Model for Beaver Pelt Price. Northeast Wildlife Vol. 55.

[60] Anonymous 1987. Historic Value of US Dollar. Mykindred.com/cloud/TX/Documents/Dollar

[61] Robert F. Gotie 1998. Fur Harvest Statistics – Update (1980-1998). Memo to Fur information Group, NYS Bureau of Wildlife, Cortland, NY, USA.

[62] Louis Sahagun and Phil Willon 2019. California becomes first state to ban fur trapping after Gov. Newsom signs law. LA Times 9/4/2019.

[63] Robert F. Gotie 1998. NY's Own Barking Dog. The New York Forest Owner, Volume 36(3) May/June.

[64] Gary Will, Mark Brown and Robert F. Gotie 1975. Northern New York Fisher Survey. Project W-130-D, W-135-D and W-136-D, Study Proposal, NYS DEC, Bureau of Wildlife, Raybrook, NY, USA.

[65] Robert Foley, Jackling, R.L. Sloan and M.K. Brown 1988. Organochlorine and Mercury Residue in Wild Mink and Otter: Comparison with fish. Environmental Toxicology and Chemistry, Vol. 7:363-374.

[66] Bruce Penrod 1976. Fisher Reintroduction Program in the Catskills. Annual Report of the Furbearer and Small Game Mammal Unit. NY Bureau of Wildlife, Delmar, NY USA.

[67] Kimberly Royer 2002. Marking the Martes Americana: Can the marten survive in Modern Vermont. View from the Vermont Fish & Wildlife Department.

[68] Dennis Money 2001. The Homecoming 1995-2001, The Story of the New York River Otter Project. Magazine published by the NYROP, Inc.

CHAPTER IV

BEAVER POPULATION MANAGEMENT (LATE 20ᵀᴴ CENTURY)

The Early Years of Organized Management

During the 1920s and 1930s, the full extent of property damage, nuisance control and management costs of having restored the beaver to New York became obvious. [1] At the end of the 1930s, Gardiner Bump and Arthur Cook, two wildlife biologists in the first Furbearer Project (W-1-R and W-34-R), boldly declared that beavers provide many benefits as well. [2] This included waterfowl production, the value of the species and its management in communicating management messages to the public, flood control and annual yields of beaver pelts. They also clearly articulated that beaver populations could be managed by fur-trapping to maintain a favorable balance of costs and benefits. (**Figure 14**) Unfortunately, it would be many years before beavers would be managed consistent with these ideas in New York State.

In the mid-forties, the Conservation Department (the Conservation Commission became a comprehensive department of state government in 1926) implemented the first statewide beaver management strategy. It identified three broad geographic areas in the

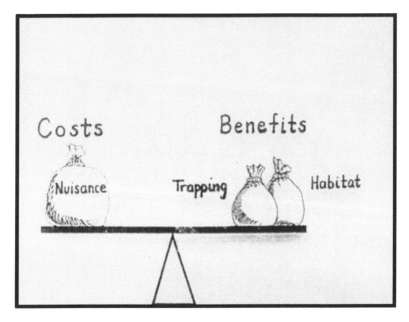

Figure 14. Legal harvest by trapping was used to balance the costs vs benefits of beavers in NY during the late 20th century.

Adapted from: Mike Ermer, Bill Sharick and Bob Gotie 2004. Trapping Matters in NY. NY Bureau of Wildlife Presentation, White Eagle Conference Center, Lake Morraine, NY

state. (**Figure 15**) Beaver harvest management goals were established for each area. [3] The first goal involved managing the harvest of beaver for sustained annual yield in counties where there was little conflict with agricultural interests. Counties comprising the Adirondacks circumscribed this management area. The second strategy objective, basically for mostly semi-agricultural counties where beaver damage was important, concentrated on maintaining a minimum sustainable beaver population. The Taconics of eastern New York, the Catskills, eastern Lake Ontario and counties west across the Appalachian Plateau of central and western New York occupied this expanse. Lastly, periodic elimination of beaver populations in the more important agricultural counties of the Lake Ontario Plains satisfied the third goal of this strategy. This initial framework for beaver management was in effect for over 40 years.

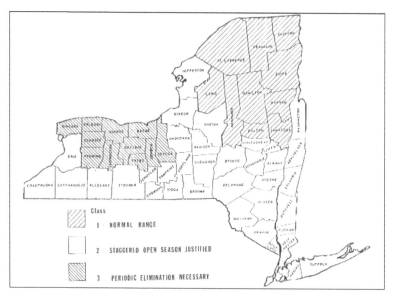

Figure 15. The 1940s saw the first objectives for managing beaver populations.

Taken from: 34th Annual Report to the NYS Conservation Department.

While the value of beaver pelts was clearly evident under this strategy, the other values of beavers, recognized as early as 1940, were not major considerations. As the Furbearer Project was combined in 1953 with a new Marsh Ecology Project (W-80-R), progress in beaver management remained one of simply reducing beaver damage complaints with little programmatic recognition of the other significant benefits of beavers. [4] Research on improving the actual management of beavers took a back seat to marsh ecology studies of small man-made ponds.

During the late 1960s, two NY Conservation Department biologists (Nathaniel R. Dickinson and Gary R. Parsons) re-examined the potential for managing beaver populations at the urging of New York trappers and sports people. The result of their work rekindled interest in the systematic management of beaver populations throughout New York. They proposed, if all benefits that beavers provide were recognized including the traditional benefits associated with fur-trapping, the cost/benefit ratio would favor higher beaver populations than could be simply justified for fur-trapping alone. To achieve the greatest good, populations would need to reach a balance between biological limitations and social constraints. They further implied information on biological and social parameters for beaver populations, techniques for determining a given population's proximity to those limits and a means for maintaining populations at desirable levels would all be needed.

Where human development is minimal, these two wildlife biologists completely understood the major limiting factor for beaver populations would be biological capacity. However, in most of the state where intensive human land use prevailed, public tolerance for beavers reaches its upper limit first.

Early in the 1980s, New York's wildlife field biologists understood all too well that higher beaver populations throughout New York in the future, and therefore more wetland benefits, required improving public tolerance for beavers. The Bureau of Wildlife began measuring the social context of beaver management beginning in the mid-1980s, when it first commissioned a study with Cornell's Human Dimensions Research Unit. Several other studies by Cornell University followed from 1987 to 2003. All delivered useful insight into understanding people's modern view of beavers and their bigger presence in New York.

A new Furbearer Project in Albany, NY (W-35-R) was initiated in the early 1970s under the leadership of Ben Tullar, a former biologist in the NY Bureau of Wildlife, Watertown, NY. The new project leader immediately began field studies on red and gray foxes, two important species in the recently emerging fur trade. [5] As the fur trade in the US began to expand, so did concern over humaneness in trapping and the growing movement of animal rights activists. Ben Tullar, keenly interested in the humaneness of trapping devices used in canine trapping, examined the differences between foot hold traps and snares, in so far as injury scores of these various traps and how they measured up. [6]

By the mid-1970s, reorganization was overtaking the NY Division of Fish and Wildlife. With it came the resulting closure of the southeastern Adirondack wildlife office, as an autonomous NY DEC Region. The NY Bureau of Wildlife at the same time saw the need to expand furbearer management beyond trap testing, as the world fur market began to go ballistic. Newer priorities were established, which meant extensive trap testing could wait. In the mid-1970s, the leadership at the NY Bureau of Wildlife in Albany, NY pulled in Gary Parsons, the former wildlife manager of the southeastern Adirondack office to take the leadership reins of the recently formed Furbearer Project. Gary Parsons was a well-known advocate for going beyond testing foot traps for humaneness. His vision was broader, more focused on strategic planning, a necessity at this time as the world market for furs expanded.

In late 1976 Parsons submitted a draft of his vision for managing all furbearing mammals with a special emphasis on beaver throughout New York. There were four major objectives targeted for the American beaver. First, maintain a statewide harvest of 7 to 11 thousand beaver annually by at least 1,300 trappers until more was known about harvest rates and distribution. Second, delineate ecological and socially homogeneous beaver management units in New York and then establish optimum harvest levels and regulations for each by 1986. Third, reduce at least by 40% the staff time spent by agency personnel on beaver damage mitigation. Lastly, describe beaver trapper behavior and preferences and use this information for making appropriate trapping season decisions. The final draft of this plan was completed two years later by the co-author in 1979. [7] To our knowledge most of the general objectives for furbearers and for beavers were completely met by the mid-1980s. A final plan for more intensively managing beaver populations throughout New York, however, took another decade to accomplish.

Wildlife Management Units

For decades the political subdivision of the state into county and town boundaries preceded the division of the state into distinct geographic regions useful for managing beaver populations. An important first step in New York's management of wildlife was the delineation of Game Range Divisions in the mid-1950s. [8] The second step taken in 1977 identified an ecosystem classification that could be used in natural resource management. [9]

Figure 16. Fur Management Units (FMUs) replaced counties for season delineation.

The division of the state into different geographic regions following the earliest work, however, applied only to New York's deer management program. It was only in the early 1980s that a group of biologists working in the wildlife field offices in northern New York divided this large geographic area into 25 ecological zones. [10] This ecological zone concept was further expanded by 1983 into the remainder of New York by biologist Nathan Dickinson based in Albany, NY. [11] Both methods basically employed distinct natural and sociological differences found throughout New York to delineate clear boundaries useful in the state's game and fur-bearing mammal management programs. New York's separation into ecological zones based on distinctions in biological and social characteristics meant the state could now manage the harvest of wildlife classified as game and furbearers according to those differences.

Wildlife Management Units (WMUs) became the essential framework of beaver management. They allowed for different approaches between distinct geographic units especially when mostly sociological distinctions warranted. [12] Beginning in 1980, the state was gradually

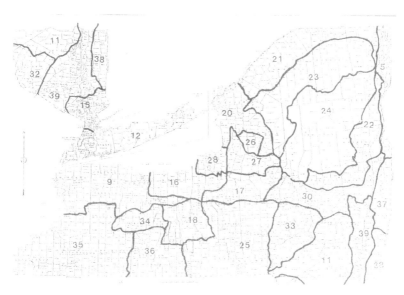

Figure 17. Wildlife Management Units (WMUs) expanded to include game and furbearers.

divided at first into twelve Furbearer Management Units (FMUs). [13] (**Figure 16**) For the first time the various beaver trapping seasons in New York followed roads of these new management units rather than county boundaries. Furbearer Management Units were further defined and expanded from the original 12 to 19 between 1980 and 1989. They were eventually renamed Wildlife Management Units (WMUs) in 1985 and now appeared in a separate map/guide. [14] Ultimately, twenty-six Wildlife Management Units (WMUs) were drawn in 1990, centered primarily on the ecological zones. [15] (**Figure 17**) Changes in management unit boundaries from the time they were initially drawn on a New York map until the authors of this document retired in 2005 have generally followed the whimsey of either regional wildlife managers or Albany area supervisors reinforcing their position of control. Trapping seasons established for a WMU overlapping two or three regional offices represented a significant threat to the autonomy of one or more mid-level supervisors who did not control the outcome. Likewise, Albany area bureaucrats required the power to make boundary changes in many cases with only their own authority in mind. The

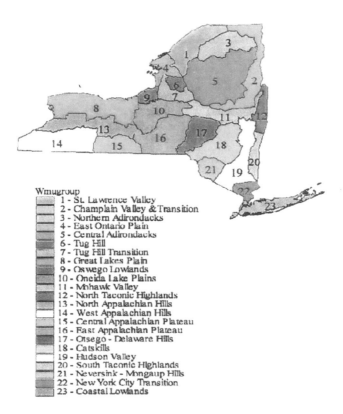

Wmugroup
1 - St. Lawrence Valley
2 - Champlain Valley & Transition
3 - Northern Adirondacks
4 - East Ontario Plain
5 - Central Adirondacks
6 - Tug Hill
7 - Tug Hill Transition
8 - Great Lakes Plain
9 - Oswego Lowlands
10 - Oneida Lake Plains
11 - Mohawk Valley
12 - North Taconic Highlands
13 - North Appalachian Hills
14 - West Appalachian Hills
15 - Central Appalachian Plateau
16 - East Appalachian Plateau
17 - Otsego - Delaware Hills
18 - Catskills
19 - Hudson Valley
20 - South Taconic Highlands
21 - Neversink - Mongaup Hills
22 - New York City Transition
23 - Coastal Lowlands

Figure 18. Aggregates of WMUs were required by changes in Deer Management Units (1998).

power struggle between adjoining NY DEC regions and Albany was a constant reminder of who really was in charge.

To ensure standardization, a set of rules for changing WMU boundaries was instituted for aquatic furbearers. These 26 WMUs stood alone for all species classified in New York as furbearers and small game, until they were altered in the late 1990s to correspond to the new alignment of Deer Management Units. Because there were over 75 Deer Management Units employed for managing deer populations in New York at this time, they had to be combined into 23 aggregates mimicking the original WMUs specified in the 1992 beaver management plan. [16] **(Figure 18)**

Original criteria specified placing unit boundaries for aquatic fur-bearers on roads, as much as possible. [17] It was completely ignored by the Regulation Revision Team who drew up the new WMU configuration. [18] Once the unit boundaries were adopted, it immediately led to an issue with central New York's Environmental Conservation Officers over the difficulty enforcing different trapping seasons on opposite banks of the Susquehanna River. The lead author at the time attempted to resolve this issue with the NY Bureau of Wildlife in Albany, NY with little success. Notwithstanding this management/law enforcement difficulty, the advent of WMUs meant that harvest management of beavers and all other furbearer and game species would now be the norm. Such a strategy for implementing emerging thoughts of an American Wildlife Management Model meant that population management by legal harvest could be tailored to the differences in population demography dictated by differences in the environment. [19]

Components of Contemporary Beaver Management

According to Webster's Dictionary, *"management is the act or art of managing, where managing means to direct, control or carry on business or affairs to achieve one's purpose."* [20] Contemporary beaver management basically stood on the shoulders of New York's previous attempts begun in the 1920s and 1940s to direct changes in beaver populations. Like the mid-1920s through the 1930s and the 1940s through the 1970s, it was built upon the premise of an annual regulated legal harvest of beavers by licensed trappers. Thus, it could be said that New York furbearer management recognized early on that furbearing mammals are a *"natural resource with measurable wealth to be sustained and managed for the benefit of present and future generations."* [21] Without the legal authority granted to the Conservation Commission in 1923, allowing private trappers to remove beaver from a large geographic area and a monetary incentive for beaver pelts, population management of this species would have merely been simple government funded pest control. [22] [23] [24] The Wildlife Services program of the Federal Animal Plant and Health Inspection Service (APHIS) utilized in the southeastern US today is a good example of how low the overall value of this important mammal has plunged

Figure 19. Too many beaver, little economic incentive for beaver pelts in the world fur market.

there. [25] (**Figure19**)

Although New York made great strides to more intensively man-age beavers during the 1980s, the approach taken was on a regional rather than statewide basis. Several wildlife field offices outside of the traditional Adirondacks, mainly northwestern, central and far west-ern New York, had already initiated beaver management plans on their own. In 1989 the newly appointed Chief Wildlife Biologist (Gary R. Parsons) empowered a group of senior wildlife biologists from the seven upstate wildlife field offices and the acting leader of the Albany, NY based Furbearer Project to advance a statewide plan for managing beavers. The structure he envisioned would be based on the ecologically and socially organized existing wildlife management units and fit New York's wildlife management mission. It would achieve maximum population levels compatible with human land use and the biological potential of the land. Its principal product would be associated recreational, economic and ecological value. [26]

This move by the chief wildlife biologist represented the first statewide NY Bureau of Wildlife sanctioned team that would soon usher in several other wildlife management teams, organized to address further vexing issues within the state. Parsons wanted to pull everyone independently working on beaver management throughout the state under the same management umbrella. Their official label at first came to be known as the NY Beaver Management Team (BMT). Five years later at the urging of the new Furbearer Project Leader, the NY Bureau of Wildlife re-named it the NY Furbearer Management Team (FMT) and directed it to address all fur bearing mammal issues of the day and into the near future. [27] (**Figure 20**) The re-named team consisted mostly of field office biologists and insofar as beaver management was concerned, were to promulgate

Figure 20. The New York Furbearer Management Team (1988-2005).

new beaver management regulations, distribute an annual report on management activities, monitor beaver populations annually through-out the state, evaluate the pelt tagging system for cost effectiveness, de-velop a beaver damage control manual, train staff to efficiently handle beaver complaints and lastly to improve damage control techniques.

Any type of management planning, whether manufacturing a new vehicle for sale or holding a population of potentially destruc-tive animals in check, follows a prescribed simple formula, similar to planning a vacation. One needs a starting location, a clear destina-tion, a means of getting there and an evaluation to determine if you arrived on station. In New York's 1990s contemporary plan for beaver management, 23 upstate WMUs existing at the time served as the foundation for this new statewide blueprint.

Plan elements consisted of four essential components. First, a po-tential habitat inventory and an annual aerial survey served as the starting location. Second, measurable population objectives linked to an acceptable occupation rate provided the destination. Third, effec-tive trapping seasons for meeting harvest goals and an accounting of the annual harvest at the end of trapping seasons achieved the method of travel. Lastly, an analysis of population change following the beaver harvest verified arrival at the correct destination. [28]

The agency cost for handling problem beavers would be de-em-phasized as the driving force in New York's strategic beaver manage-ment plan. Problems with beavers would certainly be handled as in the past, but now according to an official policy adopted by the NY Division of Fish, Wildlife & Marine.

Potential Habitat Inventory

By the early 1990s, most upstate wildlife field offices had far-reaching beaver habitat inventories. A total of 60,798 potential beaver habitat sites were accounted for in 23 of the 26 WMUs at this time. [29] The three previously mentioned inventory methods were all used in var-ious parts of New York to complete the statewide inventory. Where records were incomplete, furbearer biologists made corrections and updates on survey plots for those WMUs through the annual aerial survey. Data gleaned from these plots were then used to estimate potential sites per square mile and subsequently extrapolate the total number of potential sites in a WMU.

Annual Aerial Survey

Low-level aerial surveys conducted after leaf fall have been the traditional method for ascertaining beaver populations in New York since shortly after World War II. This method of direct observation from the air proved superior in both accuracy and cost effectiveness over early game protector ground counts of active beaver colonies in 1954. [30] Several wildlife field offices conducted this type of area wide beaver survey on an annual basis long before implementation of New York's official plan. Field biologists in all seven wildlife field offices after 1992 assumed a greater role in conducting aerial surveys than was done in the past. Stronger regional ownership of statewide beaver management was the ultimate purpose for assigning field staff to this dangerous responsibility.

The employment of the 2x3 mile survey plot was the brain child of Joseph E. Lamendola, a founding member of the original BMT. He began conducting aerial surveys in 1983 using a random sample of whole 7.5-minute USGS quadrangle maps, modeled after the surveys begun in 1981 for central New York. In the St. Lawrence Valley, whole quads proved too difficult to navigate between potential sites, because there were so many more potential sites/quadrangles than in the open terrain of south-central New York. Wildlife biologists on the BMT seeing their greater utility seized upon the smaller plots for aerial surveys throughout New York while writing the statewide beaver management plan.

The lead author and E. Michael Ermer (both original members of the BMT) first established a random cluster sampling strategy of 6 square mile plots covering 15 upstate WMUs in 1990. The sample design was meant to achieve a confidence interval estimate around the mean number of active colonies/mi^2 at p $\leq$.20 for each WMU. Since 1992, eleven WMUs were listed for annual aerial survey, where intense population management warranted the cost. Four WMUs were marked for survey every fourth year. The other eight WMUs were to be managed at such a low population density that no aerial flights were seen necessary. The original Beaver Management Team at this time calculated the cost of completing aerial surveys on a statewide basis at approximately $26,495 per year. [31] This cost included staff time as observers/navigators and rental of a suitable plane with an experienced pilot.

Closely following actual surveys in early November, active/inactive beaver colonies marked on the survey plots were counted for each WMU surveyed and then converted to active/inactive colonies/mi² with the aid of a computer spreadsheet (Microsoft Excel or Lotus 1-2-3). During the interval between 1990 and 2003 when these surveys were carried out, the annual statewide estimate of active beaver colonies numbered between 15,000 and 19,400. [32] [33] It should be noted, aerial reconnaissance did not always follow the agreed upon plan across the WMUs in New York. Safe flying weather, available staff, planes and pilots, as well as budgetary restraints all affected whether each field office completed their commitment to the plan. So, for many years between 1990 and 2003, estimates of active beaver colonies in New York are missing—the unfortunate reality of wildlife management at the state level.

Population Objectives

It has been said that wildlife management is the art of directing change to arrive at a predictable population outcome. In the case of New York's late 20th century beaver management system, population objectives for each WMU served as the outcome or destination for managers to arrive at. The proportion of potential sites actively occupied by beavers in each designated WMU was the ultimate yardstick by which success was measured. However, the more decisive metric turned out to be the number of active colonies/mi².

Potential habitat outside of the Adirondacks and Catskills continued to increase as agriculture declined over the most recent decades in New York. Under the relative and fixed objective of occupation rate, the absolute number of active colonies would proportionally increase, as the number of potential sites increased due to farmland retirement. In central New York after eight years (1990-97) of aerial survey, the number of potential sites observed increased approximately 30%. If the wildlife office had held to the original relative population objective for the nine counties, there would have been a 23.5% increase in the actual beaver population. [34] An unplanned increase of this magnitude in an area heavily populated with active farms and crisscrossed by roads would have been economically devastating to local governments and private landowners, not to mention the possible loss of regulatory authority by the state natural resource agency.

In the St. Lawrence Valley, perhaps the best beaver range in the state, the NY Bureau of Wildlife finally recognized the fixed and relative occupation rate failed to acknowledge an actual rise in the number of beaver colonies. This failure brought about a major and potentially catastrophic beaver war between the state and an escalating number of landowners suffering flooding by beavers. [35] [36] Several towns in St. Lawrence County passed resolutions sent to the NY DEC to reduce the beaver population here, putting immense political pressure on the Commissioner to examine several proposed changes in the regulations. [37] (**Figure 21**) Even the County Board of Supervi-

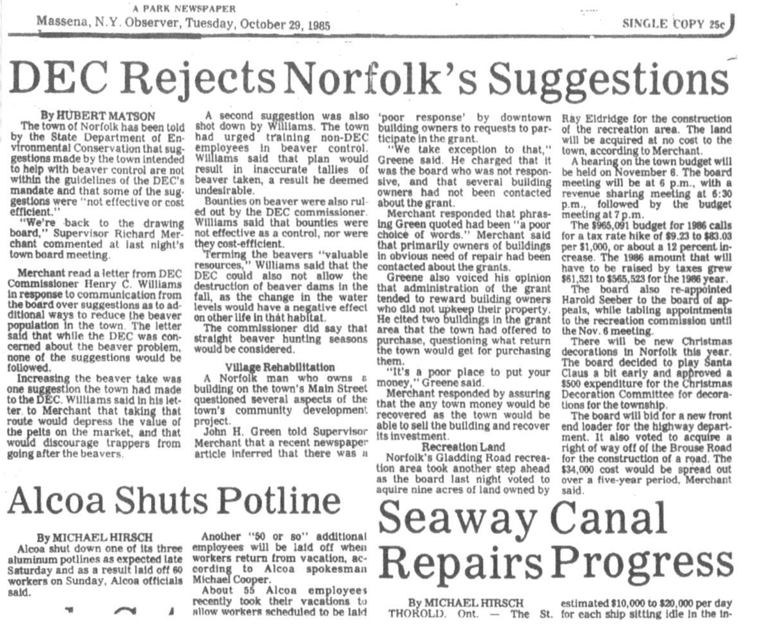

A PARK NEWSPAPER
Massena, N.Y. Observer, Tuesday, October 29, 1985   SINGLE COPY 25c

DEC Rejects Norfolk's Suggestions

By HUBERT MATSON

The town of Norfolk has been told by the State Department of Environmental Conservation that suggestions made by the town intended to help with beaver control are not within the guidelines of the DEC's mandate and that some of the suggestions were "not effective or cost efficient."

"We're back to the drawing board," Supervisor Richard Merchant commented at last night's town board meeting.

Merchant read a letter from DEC Commissioner Henry C. Williams in response to communication from the board over suggestions as to additional ways to reduce the beaver population in the town. The letter said that while the DEC was concerned about the beaver problem, none of the suggestions would be followed.

Increasing the beaver take was one suggestion the town had made to the DEC. Williams said in his letter to Merchant that taking that route would depress the value of the pelts on the market, and that would discourage trappers from going after the beavers.

A second suggestion was also shot down by Williams. The town had urged training non-DEC employees in beaver control. Williams said that plan would result in inaccurate tallies of beaver taken, a result he deemed undesirable.

Bounties on beaver were also ruled out by the DEC commissioner. Williams said that bounties were not effective as a control, nor were they cost-efficient.

Terming the beavers "valuable resources," Williams said that the DEC could also not allow the destruction of beaver dams in the fall, as the change in the water levels would have a negative effect on other life in that habitat.

The commissioner did say that straight beaver hunting seasons would be considered.

Village Rehabilitation

A Norfolk man who owns a building on the town's Main Street questioned several aspects of the town's community development project.

John H. Green told Supervisor Merchant that a recent newspaper article inferred that there was a

'poor response' by downtown building owners to requests to participate in the grant.

"We take exception to that," Greene said. He charged that it was the board who was not responsive, and that several building owners had not been contacted about the grant.

Merchant responded that phrasing Green quoted had been "a poor choice of words." Merchant said that primarily owners of buildings in obvious need of repair had been contacted about the grants.

Greene also voiced his opinion that administration of the grant tended to reward building owners who did not upkeep their property. He cited two buildings in the grant area that the town had offered to sell the building and recover its investment.

"It's a poor place to put your money," Greene said.

Merchant responded by assuring that the any town money would be recovered as the town would be able to sell the building and recover its investment.

Recreation Land

Norfolk's Gladding Road recreation area took another step ahead as the board last night voted to aquire nine acres of land owned by

Ray Eldridge for the construction of the recreation area. The land will be acquired at no cost to the town, according to Merchant.

A hearing on the town budget will be held on November 6. The board meeting will be at 6 p.m., with a revenue sharing meeting at 6:30 p.m., followed by the budget meeting at 7 p.m.

The $965,091 budget for 1986 calls for a tax rate hike of $9.23 to $83.03 per $1,000, or about a 12 percent increase. The 1986 amount that will have to be raised by taxes grew $61,521 to $565,523 for the 1986 year.

The board also re-appointed Harold Seeber to the board of appeals, while tabling appointments to the recreation commission until the Nov. 6 meeting.

There will be new Christmas decorations in Norfolk this year. The board decided to play Santa Claus a bit early and approved a $500 expenditure for the Christmas Decoration Committee for decorations for the township.

The board will bid for a new front end loader for the highway department. It also voted to acquire a right of way off of the Brouse Road for the construction of a road. The $34,000 cost would be spread out over a five-year period, Merchant said.

Alcoa Shuts Potline

By MICHAEL HIRSCH

Alcoa shut down one of its three aluminum potlines as expected late Saturday and as a result laid off 60 workers on Sunday, Alcoa officials said.

Another "50 or so" additional employees will be laid off when workers return from vacation, according to Alcoa spokesman Michael Cooper.

About 55 Alcoa employees recently took their vacations to allow workers scheduled to be laid

Seaway Canal Repairs Progress

By MICHAEL HIRSCH
THOROLD, Ont. — The St.

estimated $10,000 to $20,000 per day for each ship sitting idle in the in-

Figure 21. News account of the beginning of the beaver war in St. Lawrence County.

sors got in on the complaint. They proposed completely eliminating the legal protection on beavers in St. Lawrence County. [38] The compromise finally arrived at by both parties was for the state to make it easier to resolve issues with beavers causing problems and to reduce the population objective by recognizing the greater utility of using active colonies/mi^2 to describe the population here. With a new, more appropriate population objective in place, longer trapping seasons were established to significantly reduce the number of active colonies in this county and elsewhere.

Field biologists understood more fully that active colonies estimated directly from a statistically accurate sample survey for a unit better linked people's tolerance for the species to an absolute measure than the relative metric of occupancy rate. Furthermore, it was also more easily employed for direct estimates of beaver numbers and then used to predict next year's population in a WMU.

In the early 1990s, the original furbearer team set population objectives for 25 WMUs. About a third had objectives set at 30% of potential habitat sites occupied by an active beaver colony, another third at 20% and the last third set at 10%. [39] Adjustments were made in occupation rate objectives after the crises in the St. Lawrence Valley to actually manage New York beaver populations with the more useful objective of active colonies directly tied to new occupancy rate objectives. In most WMUs the occupation rate objective was reduced far below the biological optimum in response to the sociological imperative. When aerial survey data demonstrated stability in the number of potential sites after a few years, active colonies/mi^2 became the new normal for objectives. [40]

Setting Appropriate Trapping Season

The annual removal of surplus beavers from a population has always been considered the essence of New York beaver management. The removal of beavers since 1924 through a legal system of trapping has proven its effectiveness over the years for adjusting the size of beaver populations. Beaver trapping has also provided a means for New York citizens to economically benefit from the beaver resource.

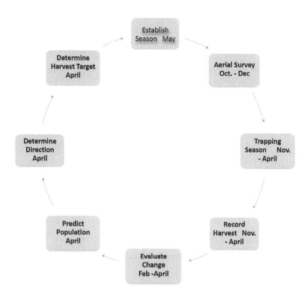

Figure 22. The 1992 NY Beaver Management Plan incorporated a season setting cycle.

Regulating the removal of beavers from a population has long involved merely the legal authority for a yearly regulatory practice. For years and sometimes decades, trapping seasons for beaver and other furbearers remained fixed until, as William Severinghaus (former Supervisor of New York's wildlife research unit in Albany) once said to the lead author in the mid 1980s, the *"squawk index becomes too loud."* In other words, when enough people leveled complaints about what they perceived as too short or too long a currently existing harvest season, the "squawk index" would set off an official state response. New York's wildlife agency would then make appropriate season changes to quell the background noise. The process designed in early 1992 essentially employed an actual annual management cycle, which was innovative for beaver management at the time. (**Figure 22**) Only white-tailed deer management possessed a similar annual progression.

The cycle began in May of each year when trapping seasons for next year were established. Under New York law, it takes several months for regulations to proceed through the legal process and then make it into the trapping guide before the trapping season opens in early winter. Aerial survey is the next step in the cycle. They would be conducted before trapping seasons began, usually in late fall. Seasonal trapping seasons, the third step, would be accessible between late November and early April of the following year. The number of beavers taken by trappers were then tallied in the fourth step from pelt seal records, within ten days after the close of the beaver trapping season. If harvest targets were not reached within the advertised season, the trapping season could be extended to harvest more beavers. Trapping seasons once again would be set in May after all pelts were tallied, evaluation (step 5) and predictions (step 6) of population change made for next year. Harvest targets for the next cycle would be established to either increase, decrease or stabilize populations in relation to the management objective (steps 7 and 8).

Annual Pelt Sealing

An accounting of the annual harvest of beavers through the attachment of recognizable tags has been a major part of beaver management since 1934. (Appendx 1) Several types of metal, cardboard and plastic tags were used for tagging harvested beaver over the years. The metal seal first used in 1934 remained in use until replaced by a cardboard tag in 1973. (**Figure 23**) At this time the NY Division of Fish and Wildlife completely took over the long-held practice from Law Enforcement for recording the harvest of New York's rarer and most important furbearing mammals.

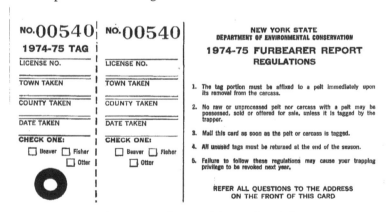

Figure 23. Paper pelt tags were first used during the 1970s.

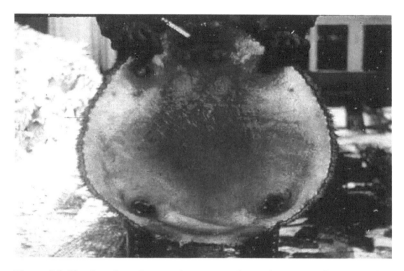

Figure 24. Plastic pelt seals came into use in the mid-1980s and continued in use until 2009-10.

The tally of beaver pelts sealed for the year was chiefly done by hand before the NY Bureau of Wildlife assumed the responsibility for the record keeping process. Such a tedious method required months of effort by regional and Albany, NY staff and usually meant that a harvest report was forthcoming many months after the next trapping season had begun. During the 1970s, computer technology leaped ahead along with newer, easier, more user-friendly software. It was in this moment that the NY Bureau of Wildlife created a separate Biometrics Unit that could now maintain records more easily and produce timely reports available for analysis long before decisions on management changes needed to be made. Eventually, with rapid advancements in computers and software by the early 21st century, nearly all field personnel finally became adept at analyzing data in a timely fashion.

Accompanying this change was the requirement for trappers to obtain a tag/report card. The report was to be filled out by the successful trapper after catching a beaver and the tag attached to the pelt. The report card was to be sent to the NY Bureau of Wildlife in Albany, NY where these report cards would be counted.

Plastic seals (**Figure 24**) came into general use for beaver, otter, fisher, marten and coyote, replacing cardboard tags and metal seals in

Figure 25. A sample of plastic pelt tags used between (1984 -2001).

1984. Plastic seals were found to be cheaper, stronger and more tamper proof. The return in 1984 to an agency person physically attaching a seal to a pelt came about due to concern by law enforcement of illegal interstate trafficking of illegal pelts. [41] The color of the plastic seals was also annually changed to not only make accounting more accurate for a given season, but also to reduce the possibility of illegal activity. Seals attached in person by wildlife technicians, wildlife biologists of the NY Bureau of Wildlife and ENCON officers continued until the 1997-98 season. (**Figure 25**) After this time, only NY Bureau of Wildlife staff officially were assigned this responsibility. However, many environmental officers throughout New York voluntarily requested a small supply of seals from the wildlife field offices. Sealing pelts of trappers kept these officers in contact with people who knew what was legally or illegally going on in the fields and forest of New York. NY Bureau of Wildlife staff were especially appreciative of this assistance.

The cost of attaching seals to pelts of five species of important New York furbearers has always concerned the administrators of the NY Division of Fish and Wildlife in Albany, NY, especially as the agency was forced at times by funding shortfalls to reduce its program's footprint. Diverting expenditures on one wildlife program to provide greater funding for a project seen as higher priority by the leadership of the NY Bureau of Wildlife is but one instance of normal operating practices of all government agencies during tough economic times. So, it has been for the accurate accounting of important and economically valuable furbearers through the pelt sealing process since the 1950s.

The placement of metal tags on beaver pelts by game protectors was halted between 1961 and 1966. No written records explaining this major change could be found. Could it have been the result of program re-prioritization and diversion of funding? Could it have been simply an administrator at the leadership level, without any ownership of the project's value to beaver management at the time, making an arbitrary decision to save money? We surmise both the law enforcement and wildlife bureaus lost interest in managing the harvest of beavers because other priorities took precedent over beaver management. Therefore, the leadership of the NY Division of Fish and Wildlife saw little need to monitor the harvest of beaver by a costly activity of placing seals on beaver pelts. This same situation beset the biologists of the Beaver Management Team, first in 1991 and again in 2001 by the NY Furbearer Management Team.

Chief Wildlife Biologist Gary Parsons in 1990 expected his furbearer biologist team at the onset to examine the continuing costs of placing pelt seals on thousands of beaver pelts. To that end, the Beaver Management Team determined the cost at $3.32/pelt sealed. The estimate included 24% extra in fringe benefits. [42] The late 20th century pelt sealing system came about in response for tighter interstate control from the states in the northeastern US. All of the states who first called for New York to implement a more secure pelt seal system demanded it continue in 1991. [43]

In 2001 the leadership of the NY Bureau of Wildlife once more called for an examination of the costs for placing seals on beaver pelts. Biologists of the Furbearer Management Team once again estimated these costs and determined it to be $3.11 including fringe benefits. [44] The actual costs had gone down, because in the early 2000s another change was made to reduce staff time and accommodate trappers' wishes while still obtaining an accurate accounting of the annual harvest. Trappers were no longer required to physically present their pelts to the wildlife staff or a conservation officer, although that option was still available. Trappers could easily obtain

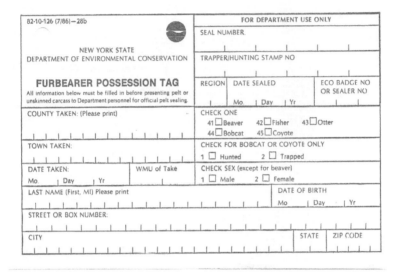

Figure 26. Furbearer possession cards were used to gather information on the harvest.

seals for their pelts by mailing their completed possession cards to the wildlife field office or the NY Bureau of Wildlife Office in Albany, NY where wildlife staff would then directly mail pelt seals to the trapper's address.

Several different methods for recording the harvest of a beaver were made between 1966 and 1985, when the NY Bureau of Wildlife assumed responsibility for the process. Beaver harvest records were recorded for just county and town until 1980 when a record of the Furbearer Management Unit where beavers were taken was added. After 1992 trappers could obtain possession cards that captured information like, who the trapper was, where he/she lived, what town/county/WMU the beaver was taken from, and the date when taken. (**Figure 26**) The seal number was written on the possession card to link the beaver pelt to the trapper.

As beaver populations increased through the 1990s, accompanied by significant increases in the annual beaver harvest by the most active trappers, accommodations were made to simplify the possession card step. A page size card designed by wildlife biologist Joseph

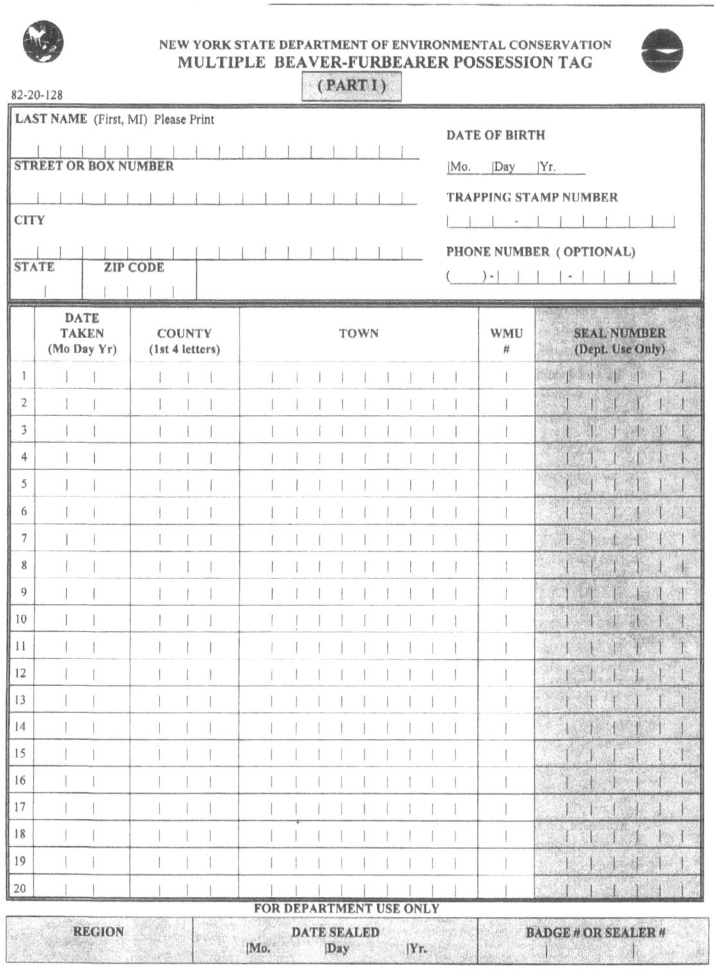

Figure 27. Multiple beaver possession report card developed in the 1990s.

E. Lamendola allowed 20 beavers to be reported per page with trapper information placed only once near the top. (Figure 27) This change made it easier for trappers to fill out possession cards and field staff to quickly assign seal numbers to the trapper.

In 2002 New York's newly created harvest reporting system, called DECALS, was adapted for pelt sealing. It now allowed trappers to report their beaver harvest by phone or interactive computer application. The information gathered each season, directly from known beaver trappers, was eventually compiled into an annual report and ultimately used to help analyze the dynamics of beaver population change in most of New York. Under this continuous, ever-evolving harvest monitoring procedure, a relatively unbroken actual accounting of the annual beaver harvest was maintained for 75 years.

It should be noted an attempt at estimating the beaver harvest using the Trapper Mail Survey was fashioned in 2000 and 2001. An examination of these estimates in conjunction with the pelt seal data by the lead author showed the mean beaver harvest estimate never came close to the level of detail and accuracy that the beaver pelt seal data achieved.[45] [46] Certainly, estimates of the harvest for the entire state could be made, but accurate estimates at the WMU level were found wanting. It was here at the WMU level where actual population regulation was accomplished. Attaching pelt seals to beaver pelts continued until 2009-10 when it was terminated, presumably because the NY Bureau of Wildlife no longer had interest in the management of beavers, nor saw it as needed.

Population Analysis

Predicted beaver populations for next year in each WMU were made using data summarized from the previous fall aerial survey and the count of beavers taken in the previous trapping season. These predicted populations would then be compared to stated objectives. Through additional modeling, harvest targets would be proposed for next year. These targets were aimed at managing populations as close to objectives as possible.

Predictive models for managing beaver populations in New York began with E. Michael Ermer working in western New York. In the early 1980s, he used ten years of aerial survey data and harvest records to establish a linear regression on harvest versus the change in the numbers of active colonies. [47] Using this regression model, he proposed that two beaver harvested per active colony stabilized a beaver population in the area he worked in. The correlation coefficient was so low, however, he did not feel confident it adequately described the dynamics of the beaver population. An analysis he later completed on age specific data portrayed as a life table revealed that most of the variation in his regression was probably due to changes in colony size.

The next model advanced was designed by the lead author for central New York during the mid-1980s. [48] New York was essentially in the business of managing a population of active beaver colonies, rather than a population of individual animals. He built a matrix model with colonies broken into three logical classes naturally occurring in nature (single, pair, family) and a 3x3 transition matrix employed to estimate next year's population of active colonies following harvest. [49] It, however, did not use locally collected data on family colony size nor proportion of single, pair and family colonies, but rather relied on published data collected elsewhere. This was seen as a significant shortcoming during the 1990s by a Cornell University doctoral candidate who developed a mathematical model incorporating beaver biology and the chronology of life events in the annual cycle of a beaver population. [50]

Michael Runge synthesized a very dynamic model for a harvested beaver population that was both complex and thorough. To field biologists, it was seen as too impractical for them to directly apply to setting annual beaver trapping seasons. Even though he suggested the number of parameters needed in his model could be considerably shortened, the level of annual detail required was never seen necessary to meet New York's statutory responsibility for managing beavers. His model's greatest strength was one of population simulation, because it clearly demonstrated and backed up observations on the most important population parameters, like adult litter and colony size.

In the end, only E. Michael Ermer's and the lead author's models were employed in a few wildlife field offices in New York. Both required only an accounting of the number of active beaver colonies and the harvest for the WMU, two parameters already being collected in several WMUs. The accuracy of these two models was also deemed sufficient for meeting New York's beaver management responsibility under the law.

The lead author used his simple model to predict the density of beaver populations between 1982 and 2002. In the 16 years with actual annual aerial survey data for the Appalachian Plateau of south-central NY, predictions using this model fell within the confidence interval estimates for the population density in 11 of these years. (**Table 4**) In four of these survey years, his predictions underestimated and in one year he overestimated the population. These predictions helped to establish clear harvest targets and prescribe the following year's trapping season. Predicted populations between years without observational data was also sometimes used to set future trapping seasons. Surveys for the years 1998, 2000, 2001 were not executed in the Appalachian Plateau because of a modification from the former annual survey plan. The change in survey frequency here was necessitated by a reassignment of two members of the survey crew, leaving all three management units to be flown by one person.

In the remainder of New York, other wildlife field offices continued to mostly hold fast to their existing seasons until the desired effect to increase, stabilize or decrease the population of active beaver colonies was achieved. Except for a few wildlife management units in New York, during the waning decade of the 20th century, little analysis of annual population dynamics occurred. [51]

Management Results

Contemporary furbearer management began seeing results under Gary Parson's leadership in the late 1970s with final completion of his strategic plan. [52] It continued into the early 1980s with the incorporation of ecological appreciation in the switch from counties to Fur Management Units and the reinstatement of a statewide small game hunter and trapper harvest survey. The new harvest survey employed telephone interviews which was an innovation at the time for the NY Division of Fish and Wildlife. [53] The Trapper and Small Game Harvest Surveys continued until the late 1990s when it was contracted to Cornell's Human Dimensions Research Unit, due mainly to a reduction in staff and the growth of home answering machines, which facilitated call screening.

Table 4. Beaver Population Statistics for the Appalachian Plateau in Central NY [1]

Fall Survey Year	Predicted # Active/mi^2	Observed # Active/mi^2	Objective # Active/mi^2	Square Miles
WMU 14				3,574
1982	None	.19 - .22	.24	
1983	.22	.20 - .23	" "	
1984	.23	.27 - .29	" "	
1985	.30	.28 - .31	" "	" "
1986	.31	.32 - .35	" "	" "
1987	.22	.23 - .26	" "	" "
1988	.24	.23 -.26	" "	" "
1989	.20	.20 -.23	" "	" "
WMU 25				4,125
1990	.23	.19 - .26	.30	" "
1991	.25	.24 - .30	.30	" "
1992	.26	.27 - .35	.30	" "
1993	.33	No Survey	.30	" "
1994	.31	.29 - .37	.30	" "
1995	.31	.25 - .35	.30	" "
1996	.28	.28 - .38	.30	" "
1997	.29	.27 - .35	.30	" "
WMU EAPP				3,139
1998	.36	No Survey	.30	" "
1999	.38	.26 - .34	.30	" "
2000	.31	No Survey	.30	" "
2001	.34	No Survey	.30	" "
2002	.29	.27 - .35	.30	" "

[1] Source: Robert F. Gotie, Annual Reports between 1982 and 2002, Fall Aerial Beaver Surveys in NYS DEC Region 7, Cortland, NY.
Between 1982 and 1989 the rate of active beaver colonies occupying a sample of the 2,674 potential beaver colony locations was used
to estimate active colonies/sq. mile. Beginning in 1990 active colonies/sq. mile was estimated from direct observation on a sample of
6 sq. mile plots in the Appalachian Plateau of Central NY.

The use of the telephone to gather information on trappers and hunters by actual wildlife field staff was replaced by a far less statistically reliable mail survey. After a time, biologists in the field offices rarely employed the data to assist in changing management actions due to the extremely wide confidence intervals about the mean harvest estimates and the length of time it took to get the results.

Fall beaver pond aerial surveys expanded in north western, eastern, central and far western NY, making it now possible to estimate the number of active beaver ponds throughout the various eco-regions in New York. Furthermore, most of the seven upstate NY wildlife field offices began applying Parsons's, Brown's and Nate Dickinson's early work on beaver habitat inventories and occupation rate by the late 1980s. Their work finally led to population objectives for all upstate wildlife management units.

Beaver populations were intentionally increased throughout the Catskill Mountains and west through the Appalachian Plateau as well as east of Lake Ontario to the central Adirondack Mountains. Various NY DEC regions also began developing their own complaint handling policies that conformed more to the policy established in the late 1930s. Translocation of problem beaver was finally laid to rest in nearly all complaint situations. The finalization of a statewide plan in 1992 for managing beaver fulfilled Gary Parsons's vision for this economically important mammal in NY.

As conflict between beavers and people increased during the 1980s and 1990s, the Human Dimensions Research Project at Cornell University was enlisted to examine the human side of beaver damage, first in central NY and then in the St. Lawrence Valley. These studies helped the NY Bureau of Wildlife to understand and then reach common ground with people aggrieved by beaver activity. Population objectives throughout the state were lowered or completely changed because of our greater understanding of the human cost of beavers. Unfortunately, as the value of pelts decreased in the face of increasing numbers of beaver through the last two decades of the 20th century, lengthening of trapping seasons became less and less effective in regulating the annual changes in the beaver population in New York.

In the last quarter of the 20th century, beaver populations rose from approximately 3,200 active beaver colonies in 1975 to a high of over 19,400 in 1994. [54] [55] The population in 1994 exceeded New York's management goal of 14,000 beaver colonies by a magnitude of 5,400 active colonies. Beavers harvested over this time period increased 250%. (**Figure 28**) However, the purchasing power of the dollar drastically declined. (**Figure 29**) Nonetheless, the percent of

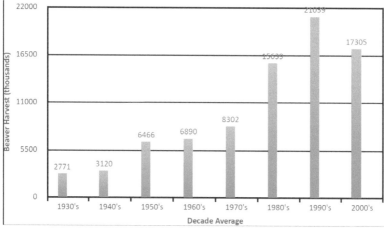

Figure 28. Average annual number of beavers harvested in New York (1930s-2000s).

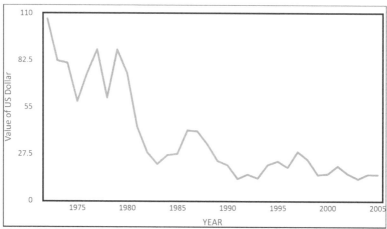

Figure 29. The Purchasing Power of a Beaver Pelt Adjusted by the value of the US dollar (Base year 2005).

successful beaver trappers nearly doubled. It seems probable that the rise in beaver harvest, as well as more successful beaver trappers, resulted from the dramatic rise in the beaver population, accompanied by substantially longer trapping seasons.

If one only looks at the dollars directly received for their beaver pelts, one would think the income of a beaver trapper had risen in the last years of the 20th century. However, using 2005 as the base year, the adjusted beaver trapper income actually experienced a two-fold decline in real dollar value between 1970 and the end of the 20th century. (**Table 5**) This distinction is important to acknowledge, because a trapper, as a consumer, now has less overall monetary value for his work expended during the trapping season. When in the early 1970s a trapper could easily catch as few as fifteen beavers in order to pay his property taxes, he/she would find it impossible to do so today. Devaluation of the dollar, however, did not completely slow down trapper interest in beaver trapping. It merely influenced a significant reduction in the total value of all wild furbearer peltries including beaver pelts. The loss of value and significant population declines in the two most economically important New York furbearers (muskrat

Table 5. Relative Trapper Income as a function of the decline in the value of the US dollar.

Year [1]	Beaver Harvest	#Beaver Trappers	Mean $/pelt	Total $ Value Unadjusted	Trapper Income [3]	Total $ Value [2] Adjusted	Trapper Income [3] Adjusted
'72-73	12,419	1,672	$18.75	$232,856	$139.26	$1,023,403	$612.08
'86-87	23,754	2,337	$24.05	$571,284	$244.45	$982,037	$420.21
'94-95	31,611	1,840	$17.99	$568,682	$309.06	$729,050	$396.22
'01-02	22,533	1,397	$14.41	$324,701	$232.43	$352,625	$252.42

[1]: *Selected the year with highest harvest in the decade to calculate total value.*
[2]: *Adjusted total value calculated with CPI Base year 2005. Mean pelt value adjusted by the value of a dollar (base year 2005) reported in mykindred.com.*
[3]: *Income /trapper calculated by dividing total value estimates by the number of beaver trappers.*

and raccoon) more than likely caused a shift to trapping more beavers by a smaller population of licensed trappers remaining in New York. (**Figure** 30) Beavers in the 1990s became more abundant and more easily accessible than in the past. Thus a $15 beaver pelt readily available in most New York townships became a more attractive target species for a trapper than a $2.00 muskrat pelt from a species becoming relatively scarce.

Landscape scale trapping through a legally prescribed trapping season had proven itself in the past to be a major factor in the dynamics of beaver populations. So, it was not unusual in the 1990s for New York biologists to greatly expand the length of beaver trapping seasons. Longer trapping seasons meant more trapper participation, and we expected greater numbers of beaver removed. Trapping license sales rose somewhat in the first few years of the 21st century, and thankfully beaver harvest and pelt values stabilized enough to cause a 17% reduction in the number of active colonies. These same

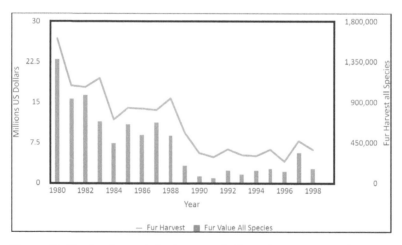

Figure 30. Total value and the harvest of all species in New York (1980-1998).

Data taken from: Robert F. Gotie 1998. Fur Harvest Statistics – Update (1980-1998).

Unpublished data, Memo to Furbearer Information Group, NY Bureau of Wildlife, Region 7, Cortland, NY, USA.

longer trapping seasons remained in effect long after most of the original biologists of the NY Furbearer Team retired. Unfortunately, biologists who replaced the original members of the FMT ceased aerial beaver pond surveys after 2005. Without these surveys each fall, New York's current biologist cadre have little ability to assess the impact longer seasons are having on beaver populations today. How many active colonies exist now and the influence of vastly expanded trapping seasons on beaver populations remains a question for the next generation of New York wildlife biologists.

In 2002, as the NYS Division of Fish, Wildlife and Marine contemplated another significant reduction in force, the NY Furbearer Management Team debated the impact to the NYS Bureau of Wildlife's mission to deliver quality wildlife research and survey work in support of important management activities they helped foster. [56] These anxious biologists offered a startling observation for the future of beaver management. Contemporary beaver management was only ten years old when the NY Furbearer Management Team eliminated meaningful population objectives for several of the original WMUs that formerly defined important wetland benefits from increased beaver activity. Population objectives were replaced and downgraded to simply minimizing beaver-human conflict or with a hollow recreational goal. In effect they envisioned a return to the past for the future of beaver management.

Although a group of furbearer biologists came together to produce a visionary strategy for managing this economically and environmentally important mammal, they for the most part failed to follow through with several elements of their original management plan. As the 21st century unfolded, it became quite clear that intensive management of beavers would soon be relegated to the trash bin of history when early retirements began to erode the ranks of the originators of contemporary beaver management.

References

[1] Gardiner Bump 1941. Problems of Beaver Management in a Fish and Game Program. 6th North American Wildlife Conference. Pp. 300-308.

[2] Gardiner Bump and Arthur Cook 1941. op. cit.

[3] 35th Annual Report of the Conservation Department New York 1944/45.

[4] 42th Annual Report 1953. op. cit., page 29.

[5] Benjamin F. Tullar,Jr and Lewis T. Berchielli ,r, 1982. Comparison of Red foxes and Gray foxes in Central New York with respect to certain features of Behavior Movement and Mortality. NY Fish and Game Jour. 29(2):127-133.

[6] Louis Berchielli, Jr and Benjamin F.Tullar,Jr 1980. Comparison of leg Snare with a Standard Leg Gripping Trap. NY Fish and Game Journal 27(1):63-71.

[7] Gary R. Parsons 1976. Strategic Plan for Beaver Management. Report to NYS Bureau of Wildlife, Regional Wildlife Managers, 11/12/76 and 12/13/76, Albany, NY, USA.

[8] R. H. Smith 1955 Definition of Game Range Divisions in New York, NY Fish and Game Journal 2(2):127-141.

[9] J.A. Davis 1977. An ecosystem classification of New York State for natural resource management. NY Fish and Game Journal, 24(2):129 – 143.

[10] Gary B. Will, Randall D. Stumvoll, Robert F. Gotie and Edward S. Smith 1982. The Ecological Zones of Northern New York. NY Fish and Game Journal 29(1):1-25.

[11] Nathaniel R. Dickinson 1983. Physiographic Zones of Southern and Western New York. Final Report W-162-R, Fed Aid in Wildlife Restoration, NYS Department of Environmental Conservation, Albany, NY, USA.

[12] Paul G. Bishop et.al. 1992. op. cit.

[13] Herbert E. Doig. NYS Department of Environmental Conservation, Hunting, Trapping and Fishing Syllabus, 1980-81.

[14] Herbert E. Doig. NYS Department of Environmental Conservation, Hunting, Trapping and Fishing Syllabus, 1985-86.

[15] Kenneth F. Wich. NYS Department of Environmental Conservation, Hunting, Trapping and Fishing Syllabus, 1990-91.

[16] Gerald A. Barnhart. NYS Department of Environmental Conservation, Hunting, Trapping and Fishing Syllabus, 1998-99.

[17] Paul G. Bishop et.al. 1992. op. cit.

[18] Richard Henry 1997. Regulations – Big Game Regulations Changes. Memo from Team Leader, Regulations Revisions Team, to NY Bureau of Wildlife, Management Team, Albany, NY, USA.

[19] John F. Organ, Robert F. Gotie, Thomas A. Decker and Gordon R. Batcheller. 1998. A Case Study in the Sustained Use of Wildlife – The Management of Beaver in the Northeastern United States. Pages 125-139 in H.A. van der Linde and M.H. Danskin, editors. Enhancing Sustainability – Resources for the Future. International Union for the Conservation of Nature and Natural Resources, Gland Switzerland.

[20] The New Lexicon – WEBSTER'S DICTIONARY of the English Language 1987. Copyright by Lexicon Publications, Inc.

[21] John F. Organ, Thomas Decker, Susan Langlois and Peter G. Mirick 1996. Trapping and Furbearer Management: Perspectives from the Northeast. Northeast Furbearer Resources Technical Committee, 33pp.

[22] Mahadev Bhat, Robert F. Gotie and Luther Keller 1993. The Impact of European Community's Humane Trapping Resolution on US Wildlife Damage Control Programs. Proceedings of the 11th Great Plains Wildlife Damage Control Workshop, Kansas City, MO, USA.

[23] Mahadev G. Bhat 1994. Troubled Fur Trade and Implications for Wildlife Damage Management. CHOICES Vol. 9, Number 4, p37-38. Published by Agricultural and Applied Economics Association.

[24] William F. Siemer, Sandra A. Jonker, Daniel J. Decker and John F. Organ 2013. Toward an Understanding of Beaver Management as Human and Beaver Densities Increase. Human-Wildlife Interactions 7(1):114-131.

[25] Bromley, P. T., J.F.Heisterberg, W. T. Sullivan, P.W. Sumner, J.C. Turner, R. D. Wickline and D.K. Woodard 1994. Wildlife Damage Management – Beavers. North Carolina Cooperative Extension Service, Publication AG-472-4, North Carolina State University, Raleigh, NC, USA.

[26] Paul G. Bishop 1989. Summary of First Meeting of the Beaver Management Team (BMT). Memo to NYS DEC Biologists Team Members, Furbearer Project, Albany, NY, USA.

[27] Gordon Batcheller 1994. Expanding the Original Beaver Team to a Fur Management Team. NYS DEC, Bureau of Wildlife, Fur Project Leader, (W-173-G), Albany, NY, USA.

[28] Paul G. Bishop et.al. 1992. op. cit.

[29] Paul G. Bishop et.al. 1992. op. cit.

[30] Arthur H. Cook 1954. op. cit.

[31] Paul G. Bishop et.al. 1992. op. cit.

[32] Gordon Batcheller 1995. The 1995 Update on NYS Beaver management Program. NY Bureau of Wildlife Publication, Albany, NY, USA.

[33] Robert F. Gotie 2004. Beaver Data Summary for New York. Unpublished data, Furbearer Team Report. NYS Bureau of Wildlife, Region 7, Cortland, NY, USA.

[34] Robert F. Gotie 1998. Addendum to the 1992 Beaver Management Plan for Central NY. Memo to James Glidden and staff, NYS Department of Environmental Conservation, Bureau of Wildlife, Region 7, Cortland, NY, USA.

[35] Joseph E. Lamendola 1985. Norfolk Town Board Meeting, St. Lawrence County. Memo to Dennis Faulknham, Regional Wildlife Manager, NY Bureau of Wildlife, Region 6, Watertown, NY, USA.

[36] Leigh M. Blake 1985. Over Population of Beavers in the Town of Pierrepont, St. Lawrence County. Letter to Town Board, Natural Resources Supervisor, NYS DEC, Region 6, Watertown, NY, USA.

[37] Gary R. Parsons 1986. Meetings on St. Lawrence County Beaver Problems. Memo to Commissioner H.G. Williams, NYS DEC, Chief Wildlife Biologist, Bureau of Wildlife, Albany, NY, USA.

[38] Phyllis W. McCall 1994. Letter to Commissioner Thomas Jorling, NYS DEC: Requesting Elimination of Legal Protection for Beavers. Deputy County Clerk, 4/15/954, St. Lawrence Co. Board of Supervisors, USA.

[39] Paul G. Bishop et.al. 1992. op. cit.

[40] Robert F. Gotie 1998. op. cit.

[41] Robert A. Van Benschoten and Kenneth F. Wich 1983. Furbearer Pelt Tagging Procedures for Implementation in 1983-84. NYS DEC Divisions of Law Enforcement and Fish, Wildlife & Marine, Memo to ENCON Officers and Wildlife Staff, Albany, NY, USA.

[42] Paul G. Bishop et.al. 1992. op. cit.

[43] Mark K. Brown 1991. Furbearer Pelt Sealing. Unpublished Report of the Mid-West Furbearer Workshop, Aurora, NE, USA.

[44] Mark K. Brown 2002. Pelt Sealing Evaluation Report 2000-2001. NYS DEC, Bureau of Wildlife, unpublished report, Region 5, Warrensburg, NY, USA.

[45] 1999-2000 Mail Survey of Trappers. HDRU, Cornell U., Ithaca, NY, USA.

[46] 2000-2001 Mail Survey of Trappers. HDRU, Cornell U., Ithaca, NY, USA.

[47] E. Michael Ermer 1988. Unpublished Data for Northern Alleghany County–Linear Regression Equation. In Progress in Beaver Management in New York State. Robert F. Gotie, E. Michael Ermer, Mark K. Brown and Paul G. Bishop 1988, unpublished manuscript, NYS DEC, Bureau of Wildlife, Region 7, Cortland, NY, USA.

[48] Robert F. Gotie 1983. BPOP – A Beaver Population Model for Central New York. NYS Department of Environmental Conservation, Fed. Aid in Wildlife Restoration, unpublished Final Report, Project W-137-D, Cortland, NY, USA.

[49] Michael C. Runge 1999. Design and Analysis of a Population Model for Beaver (*Castor canadensis*). Cornell Biometrics Unit Technical Series BU-1462, Cornell University, Ithaca, NY, USA. 29pp.

[50] Michael C. Runge 1999. Design and Analysis of a Model for Adaptive Harvest Management of Beaver (*Castor canadensis*). Ph.D. Dissertation, Cornell University, Ithaca, NY, USA.

[51] Robert F. Gotie 2004. Statewide Beaver Data Summary. Unpublished Data, NYS DEC, Bureau of Wildlife, Region 7, Cortland, NY, USA.

[52] Mark K. Brown 1979. A Strategic Plan for Furbearer Management in New York. Unpublished Report, NYS DEC Federal Aid in Wildlife Restoration (W-135-D) NY Bureau of Wildlife, Warrensburg, NY, USA.

[53] Robert F. Gotie, Gary R. Parsons, E. Michael Ermer and James A. Fodge 1984. A Telephone Survey of Small Game Hunters and Trappers as a method for obtaining reliable and timely estimates of the harvest. NY Fish and Game Journal. Vol. 31, No. 2.

[54] Paul G. Bishop, Mark K. Brown, Russel. Cole, E. Michael Ermer, Robert F. Gotie, Joseph E. Lamendola, Bruce Penrod, Scott Smith and William Sharick 1994. Assessment of the Potential Effects of a Projected Beaver Population Increase. NYS Department of Environmental Conservation, Division of Fish and Wildlife, Special Report, Albany, NY, USA.

[55] Gordon Batcheller 1995. op. cit.

[56] Robert F. Gotie 2002. Future of the Furbearer Management Team. Memo to Chief Wildlife Biologist John T. Major, NYS Bureau of Wildlife, Region 7, Cortland, NY, USA.

CHAPTER V

CONTROL OF BEAVER DAMAGE

Policy Changes

In spite of the knowledge gained regarding the costs of re-establishing beaver populations in the Adirondacks, continued flooding and tree damage by beaver activity led to a new approach by the Conservation Department. From 1932 to 1938 more than 600 beavers were captured alive and relocated throughout the semi-agricultural counties of New York using a special truck known as the *"beaver bus."* [1] (**Figure 31**)

By the late 1930s the Conservation Department's tolerance with the issue of beaver damage was at a problematic level in much of New York. The Commission recognized it could no longer afford to provide complete beaver damage abatement services. The official beaver relocation program ended and a formal statewide policy of beaver damage control was developed. Game protectors would investigate beaver problems, advise on their solution, assist in destroying dams and where necessary issue permits to private landowners to destroy offending animals. The onus for most damage control action was to be shifted to the landowner. Removal of problem beaver by the state would be carried on only as necessitated by public pressure. [2]

While the program for relocating nuisance beaver officially ended, in actual practice relocation of problem beaver by State personnel

LEGEND

○ ORIGINAL STOCK — 1900

▲ INTRODUCTIONS — 1900-1910

★ REDISTRIBUTION OF POPULATION

○ DAMAGE COMPLAINT LOCATION

Figure 31. Trappers using the "Beaver Bus" released hundreds of beavers between (1932-38).

Adapted from: Gardinar Bump and Arthur Cook 1941. Black Gold—The story of the beaver in New York. NY Bureau of Game. Bulletin No. 2.

continued into the 1980s. Relocating problem beavers completely ended in central New York in 1984 despite objections by staff who performed this service for most of their careers. [3] To some extent this may have been due to a traditional mind set among field staff that beavers were valuable or rare in the eyes of New Yorkers, and it was publicly unacceptable to merely destroy offending animals. Furthermore, the state was largely viewed as responsible for the re-establishment of beavers in New York.

Many Department staff at the bio-political rank believed it should also be responsible for property damages caused by beavers. [4] Assigning a wildlife technician to live trap beavers reduced the political stress to those in quasi-political positions, more so than an effective damage policy. This obligation to save problem beavers by the Conservation Department, though, seemed rather odd in light of the underlying basis behind liberalizing beaver trapping regulations in the first place. [5]

Like their predecessors in the Adirondacks before them, the wildlife field office in far western New York discovered relocation brought about significant increases in beaver populations, where beavers were previously absent or scarce. Tag returns from relocated beavers also revealed they often did not remain at release sites and sometimes even caused a second property damage complaint. [6] The co-author serving in the southern Adirondacks found only a quarter of relocated problem beavers were subsequently harvested at release sites. [7] These formal study results argued against continuing the practice of relocating problem beavers.

In 1970, the New York Conservation Department became the New York Department of Environmental Conservation (DEC). The former had dealt primarily with fish, wildlife, forest management and law enforcement. The new Conservation Department now encompassed broader environmental responsibilities as well. A new generation of wildlife biologists coming on board through the 1970s began looking critically at beaver damage complaint policies. Biologists now, unlike the previous generation, focused their attention on reducing staff time handling beaver damage problems and using wildlife technicians for research and survey work.

Directed increases in beaver populations across central and southwestern New York resulted in subsequent increases in damage complaints during the 1970s and 1980s. At the same time the Department's focus shifted toward added environmental responsibility, forcing wildlife field offices to significantly decrease their traditional beaver damage control workload. For as long as beavers occupied land in New York, it was game protectors, rangers and wildlife field personnel who carried the burden of handling beaver damage complaints. Records maintained during this time showed that resolving beaver human conflicts accounted for nearly 75% of the total management outlay for this species. [8] Not only were complaints becoming too numerous to handle intensively, but realistically there were fewer suitable places left in New York to move problem beavers without creating more problems.

Section 200 of the New York Fish and Wildlife Law became effective on February 2, 1960. It gave the Conservation Department permanent authority to issue permits to take problem beaver in the

northern zone of New York. This law was the precursor of Environmental Conservation Law 11-0521 that expanded this authority to
the entire state. [9]

As a result, wildlife field offices independently began developing
beaver damage complaint policies more in line with what the Environmental Conservation Law (ECL) authorized. The lead author in
the early 1980s wrote a formal beaver complaint handling policy for
wildlife staff in the nine counties of central New York. [10] Eventually
with minor tweaking it became the accepted statewide standard for
the New York Bureau of Wildlife in 1991. [11] The NYS DEC led by
wildlife field staff finally did what had been attempted in the late
1930s. It moved from relocating problem beaver to investigating
problem locations and issuing permits to destroy offending animals
under ECL section 11-0521 and to remove beaver dams under ECL
11-0505. By adopting a standard handling policy, wildlife staff effort
managing beaver damage complaints across New York State was reduced by more than two-thirds. [12]

Early in 1987, as the number of problems with beaver began dra-
matically increasing, the NYS Division of Fish, Wildlife and Marine
established a new policy allowing the sale of beaver pelts taken on
beaver damage permits. [13] It was done in an effort to better utilize
the numerous pelts of beavers being taken on problem locations. Before this year all beaver killed on ECL 11-0521 permits needed to be
buried and their economic value lost.

By the mid-1990s, wildlife staff in central New York completely
ended field investigations due to a 25% reduction in wildlife field
staff caused by early retirements. [14] People with beaver damage complaints needed only to call the wildlife field office, explain their issue
and provide location information. Field staff would then automati-
cally issue a permit to remove beaver dams and to destroy offending
animals in most situations. Problems involving multiple landowners,
DEC lands, complainant requests for assistance, when directed by a
supervisor or when requested by an ENCON officer, still required a
field visit. In 1997 the NY Furbearer Management Team debated
changes in the policy of 1991 and submitted these changes to the
Chief Wildlife Biologist for approval. [15] By 2001, little action had yet

been taken by the leadership of the Bureau of Wildlife to make these needed changes. [16] Nonetheless, handling of problem beavers in person would forever be deemphasized at the regional level, as the driving force in the state's overall beaver management strategy. Certainly, problem beavers would still be handled, but now according to regional needs and priorities.

Regulations Under ECL Article 15/24

In 1975 the Freshwater Wetlands Act became Environmental Conservation Law (ECL) Article 24 in New York. It took the Environmental Department another decade to enact specific regulations under this law and another to fully begin to address the conflict between the regulation of removing beaver dams in wetlands larger than 12.4 acres ($\sim$ 5 hectares) and ECL Article 11-0505. The Bureau of Game/Wildlife had been authorizing landowners and highway departments to remove or breach beaver dams under Conservation Law since 1913, without regard to the size of the wetlands they modified. Under ECL Article 15/24 permit regulations an aggrieved landowner not only had to obtain a permit under ECL 11-0505, but also another permit under either the wetlands or stream protection law. [17]

To the wildlife biologists of the NY Furbearer Management Team, ECL Article 24 regulations dealing with removal of beaver dams made no sense, nor was seen necessary at all, [18] since beavers utilize appropriate topographic sites with a dependable water supply and woody vegetation adapted to wetland and or mesic soils. [19] [20] In effect a beaver's pond building activity for the most part simply modifies a pre-existing wetland. Beaver dams create ponded wetlands in such former sites as wet shrub and/or wooded wetlands

Removal of a beaver dam merely reverses a ponded wetland to an earlier successional stage. It does not change the fact that this piece of ground remains a wetland. After a few years, plant succession begins again and the wetland plant community slowly returns to where it was before beaver flooded it. It didn't matter to the furbearer biologists if intentionally done by man, or because the beavers moved out on their own, or were trapped during the season. They concluded it would still remain a wetland and regulated under the law, if larger than 12.4 acres.

The lead author in his 1984 study in central New York using the New York State Freshwater Wetlands Inventory essentially confirmed this fact. New York's wetland inventory identified wetlands by interpretation of hydric and mesic vegetation on 1968 air photos. Nearly all potential beaver habitat sites documented in the nine counties of central New York were identified by using the NYS Freshwater wetland vegetation maps coupled to topographic features. In a follow-up field check of 100 randomly selected known active beaver ponds in the original inventory area, he found an 86% to 93% (p≤.05) rate of coincidence with previously unoccupied wetland habitat. [21] In other words, beavers did not create the wetland. They merely modified a pre-existing one.

Furbearer Team biologists strongly suggested it would be simpler to eliminate the regulation than subject private citizens to redundancy under two separate permitting laws. After all, NY Environmental Department staff in the Bureau of Wildlife still reviewed beaver dam removal under ECL Article 11-0505 from a private landowner's cost/benefit perspective, balanced against the likelihood that it would jeopardize wetlands protection in New York.

In the end, the NY Division of Fish, Wildlife and Marine office in Albany without fanfare directed all field offices to use the new General Permit (GP-93-02) developed in 1993 for wetlands and protected streams occupied by beavers, complete with extra responsibilities for wildlife field personnel to enforce. [22] The general permit eliminated the 11-0505/11-0521 permit forms the furbearer biologists had been using specifically keyed to beaver damage and in use for at least a decade. Most of the wildlife field offices either ignored the new permit process or modified it to eliminate the redundancy. Some biologists went so far as to flatly state to the central office staff person delivering the new forms, *I will not even remove the plastic wrap on this worthless ream of permit forms."*

In central and northern New York, wildlife staff took a much different and less defiant approach. [23] According to part 663.4 of the wetland regulations, exempt activities included all agriculture including timber as a crop, roads, culverts, bridges, utility right-of-way, individual septic systems, wells, dams, dikes and other functional structures. Using this interpretation, staff handling a beaver problem location for the most part didn't need to do anything more than issue an 11-0505 permit. If a problem was found to be in a non-exempt regulated wetland, they simply wrote on the official General Permit forms, *"See attached 11-0505 permit,"* stapled it to the 11-0505 permit and sent them on their way. They also informed private landowners by writing on this new permit form, *"If using machinery to remove the beaver dam in a regulated wetland a separate application and review through the NY DEC Division of Regulatory Affairs was required."*

Notwithstanding this issue over redundant laws, the NY Bureau of Wildlife in its field offices through the end of the 20th century and into the early 21st century continued to expeditiously issue ECL Article 11-0505 permits, unencumbered by additional red tape to help private landowners solve their issue with beaver flooding. Such advocacy by late 20th century wildlife biologists was typical and totally in keeping with the traditions of their mid-century predecessors.

Pond Levelers

Early attempts to reduce impacts of beaver damage, besides moving problem beavers, also involved improving electrical shock deterrents developed in the 1950s and 1960s. [24] Although these improved devices showed promise, they were sometimes extremely vulnerable to theft and vandalism. (**Figure 32**) Because of this, emphasis shifted to improving on sluice-type water level control devices, first introduced in New Hampshire. [25] Staff in New York improved upon the New Hampshire model with several innovations to these water level control devices in the mid-1980s and 1990s. [26] [27] [28] (**Figure 33**) Numerous locations where different designs of these devices were employed showed, for the most part, these devices only function until beavers discover how to defeat their purpose by burying them with mud and sticks or building new dams downstream. (**Figure 34**) In some cases, they failed to work entirely, or as short as a few days or weeks without regular maintenance. [29]

Although most wildlife field staff in the late 20th century had significant misgivings with pond levelers, some staff in the NY DEC Di-

Figure 32. Electric shockers as a preventive measure at road culverts did not prove reliable.

Figure 33. The deep-water fence helped to guard road culverts from beaver activity.

Figure 34. This pond leveler failed after a few weeks when beaver built a dam downstream.

vision of Environmental Permits during the first decade of the 21st century did not. The Victory Highway Department, attempting to remove a beaver dam interfering with a town highway, were told after applying for a wetlands permit that removing the beaver dam was not recommended. The permit administrator declared removing the dam would impact the wetlands and the dam was trapping sediments. Furthermore, the Highway Department should coordinate with the Division of Fish, Wildlife and Marine to install blocking or a pond leveler at the culvert. [30] For the authors of this narrative, who both had years wasting time and money installing pond levelers, this kind of over reach by the NY DEC, especially on a town government department responsible for maintaining a highway, was unbelievable. It seems the bureaucratic machine of the NY DEC had become actively involved with handling beaver-human conflicts in the 21st century, a responsibility the NY Bureau of Wildlife had sole custody for more than 75 years.

In a more innovative use of pond levelers, a fisheries biologist with the assistance of the wildlife field office in Cortland, NY modified a pond leveler to allow migrating salmon to pass by a beaver dam on Orwell Brook, a tributary to the Salmon River. It was crushed after only a few days by vandals looking to exploit the numerous migrating salmon stacked up at the base of this dam. To be fair, before this leveler was demolished, it passed hundreds of migrating fish by the dam and into the upper stretch of this important tributary. However, not enough time passed to seriously analyze the effectiveness of this modified leveler to permit fish travel beyond the beaver dam.

A similar issue with beaver dams and Walleye migration in Scriba Creek, a main tributary to Oneida Lake, was partially solved, not with pond levelers, but by providing current active dam locations identified on aerial survey maps to the Constantia Walleye Hatchery. Staff at the hatchery contacted landowners in the area to request permits for dam removal and arranged permission for trappers to take beavers during the trapping season. In the waning years of the 1990s, as reductions in wildlife field staff became the norm, installation of water control devices for solving beaver problems was mostly abandoned by NY wildlife personnel. Private organizations like Beavers,

Wetlands and Wildlife still heavily promote them on their Internet site as an effective non-lethal method for solving a problem with beavers.

Road Culverts

An early study of beaver issues with road culverts was completed on the Penn Central Rail Road between Thendara, NY and Tupper Lake, NY by the lead author and the NY Department of Transportation in the summer of 1975. [31] This rail line through the heart of the Adirondack Mountains had been abandoned for many years and was recently acquired by the NY Department of Transportation. Their plan was to renovate the rail line for a future scenic rail road.

Rail bed washouts were numerous, requiring multiple trips forward and back to the trailer with the motorized handcart. (**Figure 35**) Most of the drainage streams were provided with multiple small drain tubes, which was typical of the method for drains for rail beds when this rail road was built in the 1800s. (**Figure 36**) They were simply too easy for beavers to plug them with mud, sticks and debris.

Figure 35. Serious damage to the future Adirondack RR caused by beaver activity (1975).

Figure 36. Survey along the Adirondack Railway 1975.

At the time of this rail road construction, beavers were absent from nearly all of the Adirondack Mountain Region. Road construction companies in the 1800s built their rail grades without any thought of future issues with beavers. Recommendations in this report suggested repair at these drainage streams utilize single oversize culverts and heavy stone ballast instead of the naturally occurring sand.

During the 1980s, the Bureau of Wildlife commissioned a study with the State University of New York College of Environmental Science and Forestry to test beaver pheromone-based repellents for use at road culverts. Bio-chemical communication in beavers suggested a possible solution for preventing beaver activity at suitable road culverts and small bridges. [32] [33] While this approach met with some success experimentally, it never proved to be a practical control alternative.

In the late 1990s, the NY Bureau of Wildlife became interested in examining site characteristics of road culverts to determine what, if any, features could be modified to prevent a culvert from becoming a beaver problem. Cornell Cooperative Extension Service initiated just such a master's degree study in 1997. [34] Their findings eventually revealed two variables having the most influence on beaver activity at road culverts: culvert inlet opening area and stream gradient. The conclusion of this innovative study suggested that, *"Installing oversized culverts would have the greatest influence on discouraging beaver plugging activity* at these sites." [35] Some wildlife field offices, especially in northern New York, began working more closely with town, county and state highway departments after this study was concluded to identify culvert locations where larger culverts would work.

Human Dimensions

A formal study to measure public tolerance of beaver damage and people's perception of damage costs was first initiated by the NY Bureau of Wildlife's field office in central NY in the mid-1980s through Cornell University's Human Dimensions Research Unit. [36] [37] Findings of these studies showed that beaver site owners tolerated a fair amount of occupancy by this pond building mammal, even after a major increase in beaver populations. Most site owners also perceived some value from beavers. Some landowners and highway department officials distressed by flooding, plugged culverts and tree damage, were willing to undertake long-term solutions to beaver problems including habitat modification. Nonetheless, further human dimensions studies also stressed tolerance of beaver damage decreases as perceived damage increases. [38]

Other findings from these studies indicated that preference for lower beaver populations escalates for those who experience a problem with beavers. People experiencing beaver damage problems also supported more invasive actions, like trapping and dam removal, than those with little to no interaction with beavers. These human dimensions studies in the 1980s represented the first significant attempt to fully understand people's attitudes about beavers. Similar studies in northern New York during the early 1990s further expanded New York's knowledge about people and their attitudes toward the Amer-

ican beaver. In the St. Lawrence Valley where actual beaver populations exceeded New York's population objective by more than dou-
ble, people in this important wetland region, *"generally desired lower
beaver populations even at the expense of reducing the number of potential beaver related benefits."* [39] It is interesting to note that much
of what we learned from these contemporary studies of people and
beavers can be clearly traced back to Charles E. Johnson's study of
Adirondack beavers. People either see beavers as interesting and
beneficial or consider them an unnecessary problem that needs to be
removed, especially when beavers occupy large swaths of the landscape in great numbers. Although written for an audience about to re-
volt against tyranny, Thomas Payne nearly 250 years ago expressed it
best and most germane to the issue of beavers today when he wrote
these famous words, *"What we obtain too cheaply, we esteem lightly.
It is only dearness (rarity) that gives things value."* [40]

Soon after the crises with beaver in the St. Lawrence Valley, New
York amended the statewide beaver management plan. It called for
substantially decreasing the number of beaver colonies in this important area of northern New York. The link between the number of
beaver colonies and the number of problem locations had long been
appreciated, but not mathematically proven until the mid-1990s. The
lead author in an unpublished data set covering the contiguous wildlife management units of central and northwestern New York produced a linear regression with a correlation coefficient of .96 between
the number of active colonies/mi^2 and the number of problem loca-
tions/mi^2. [41] Michael C. Runge (PhD candidate at Cornell Univ.) re-
fined the lead author's data set in 1997 with a logarithm/quadratic
function and demonstrated a much tighter linear fit with a similar
correlation coefficient, thus proving that the greatest influence on
beaver damage locations lies with the number of active colonies. [42]

New York biologists already knew from earlier studies that manipulation of the trapping season could influence the legal removal of
beavers and thus increase or decrease a population of beavers in a defined geographic area. Thus, beaver trapping seasons were lengthened
by several months throughout most of New York in 1994-95 giving
fur trappers the time they needed to take significant numbers of

beaver. [43] In 1995, one year after a significant increase in the beaver harvest, damage locations fell 7% in the St. Lawrence Valley. According to wildlife biologist Joseph Lamendola, this was the largest single year decline in the history of record keeping here. [44] In the remainder of New York, wildlife biologists also established beaver population objectives at or below optimum sustainable levels to balance the heavy costs of too many beavers.

Cornell Researchers in the 1980s and 1990s also confirmed that most people in New York did not fully understand the true value of beavers nor how the state manages them. They suggested the NY Bureau of Wildlife could do a better job of instructing its citizens on these subjects by finding new ways for direct communication. While Cornell's Human Dimensions Research Unit continued to study and publish their findings, the NY Bureau of Wildlife commenced holding public meetings, writing popular articles on beaver management to help educate New Yorkers about furbearer management. [45] [46] [47] Biologists in the field offices began giving seminars at conferences, organized trapper/sportsmen association meetings, bird clubs/nature centers and public hearings. [48] [49] [50] [51]

A complete and illustrated booklet on controlling beaver damage at problem locations was published by the NY DEC and is still in use today. [52] People interested in beavers can also find plenty of information on how to prevent or control flooding and tree damage on the NY DEC Internet Web Site.

Linking people suffering real or perceived issues with beavers and a major stakeholder group long utilized by the state to help manage beaver populations was also a specific message to the NY Bureau of Wildlife. The lead author in central New York took this suggestion seriously and for years made direct mailings to both beaver trappers and beaver damage complaints before the annual fur trapping season. [53] Although this action increased wildlife staff involvement at a busy time of year, it accomplished a great deal of good will among trappers and landowners in central NY.

In the early 1980s, the NY Division of Fish and Wildlife instituted a new program permitting private individuals to act as paid Animal

Damage Control Agents for people with a wildlife conflict. The program consolidated ECL Articles 11-0507, 11-0511, 11-0513, 11-0521, 11-0523 and 11-0505 and formalized regulations under 6NYCRR Part 175. [54] Administered by a Special License Unit in Albany, NY and first led by Chief Wildlife Technician George Teidman, it was called the Nuisance Wildlife Control License. It spawned a new private service industry in New York for those people with knowledge about Fish and Wildlife Law and the skill for solving conflicts between wildlife and people. All seven upstate wildlife field offices put this program to work on beaver damage problems by maintaining current lists of licensed agents who also had the skills necessary to handle beaver damage control work. People experiencing problems with beavers could easily obtain a permit from the state wildlife office to remove beavers and destroy their dams, and for a reasonable fee hire a licensed animal damage control person as their agent.

Knowledge gained from the social research in the 1980s to 2000s on the human side of beaver management eventually led New York's biologists to more proactively manage beaver populations for multiple values throughout the state. Furthermore, understanding the human side of wildlife management helped the NY Bureau of Wildlife to recognize the need for appropriate population objectives and subsequent management actions for most of the problematic wildlife species in New York.

Cable Snares

The prohibition on using wire or cable snares for trapping beavers traces its roots back to the laws of 1904. However, the re-codification of this law throughout the history of change in the NY DEC permitted exceptions to the general prohibitions on certain trapping devices, especially in beaver damage situations. New York Environmental Conservation Law (ECL) Article 11-1101[5] specifically bans the use of snares except with respect to destructive or menacing wildlife. During the late 1990s and early 2000s, political pressure was brought to bear on the NY Division of Fish and Wildlife by both the New York State Trappers Association and the Wildlife Damage Control Alliance to authorize wire/cable snare use in beaver damage situations where the state issues an ECL Article 11-0521 permit.

Wildlife biologists closely working on the NY River Otter Project and those in other wildlife field offices clearly saw snares as an additional tool for reducing inadvertent mortality of otters in commonly employed traps for taking problem beavers. Bowing to both outside pressure and total acceptance of snare use by field staff, the NY Division of Fish and Wildlife reworked the exception clause under ECL Article 11-0521 authorizing snare deployment on permits issued in beaver damage locations. [55]

With the new policy in effect, wildlife biologists on the statewide Furbearer Management Team implemented a training and certification program for wildlife damage control trappers in 2002. Each wildlife field office contributed to an educational pamphlet on snares and snaring, established hands-on seminars and prepared a training video to certify a future crop of well-trained wildlife control trappers. [56] Animal control agents were required to obtain this training before they could be certified to use snares under ECL 11-0521 permits. By the year 2005 many beaver damage control trappers throughout upstate New York regularly employed snares to remove beavers from problem locations.

Alternatives for Managing Beaver – Human Conflict

The NY Bureau of Wildlife field offices historically directed nearly 50% of its entire wildlife management program toward solving human-wildlife problems. This in spite of the fact only about 5-15% of a given species population causes human wildlife conflict. In advance of an impending loss of experienced wildlife biologists and technicians, the NY Furbearer Management Team recommended to the leadership that handling of problem wildlife in New York be contracted to the USDA Animal, Plant and Health Inspection Service, Wildlife Services Program. [57] With fewer anticipated wildlife staff after 2005, it would free up the remaining wildlife staff to devote their time to research and management issues of higher priority than personally handling problem wildlife.

As expected, the NY Bureau of Wildlife leadership merely reiterated what was already known: *"Interaction with the public around nuisance wildlife issues remains an important part of the Bureau's mission."* [58] However, they did not offer any real solution to the agencies' dilemma of fewer staff to handle problem wildlife while keeping relevant with scientific wildlife management. Promises about a comprehensive examination of the impact of staff reductions, the ability to deliver science-based management programs, costs and capacity of the USDA Wildlife Services Program to provide their services, as well as satisfying our nuisance customer base, sounded hollow to the biologists of the FMT. Most of these biologists and technicians had more than 30+ years of state government service and understood fully what the real meaning of comprehensive is in a government agency. By 2005 half of the biologists of the original NY Furbearer Management Team had retired, yet nothing further on this issue had been accomplished by the leadership of the NY Bureau of Wildlife.

Statewide Record Keeping

Complaints of beavers damaging property have been marked by sporadic record keeping from the earliest days of their recovery in New York to the beginning of the 1980s. The early years in the writings of the Annual Reports by the Conservation Commission speak volumes about the conflict between beavers and people, but little information was published on exactly how many individual problem locations there were. The only early numerical records of beavers causing problems with landowners were found in the 9th Annual Report of the Conservation Commission. Rangers and game protectors reported in a table 587 beaver dams flooding 8,681 acres with 70% of the dams on state-land. [59] It was a simple report by Commission employees of beaver dams that were flooding forests on private land and the Forest Preserve. Nineteen years after the first open beaver trapping season held in 1924, there were still no numerical records published either as a separate sentence or within a table in these annual reports. Not until 1942 does one see in the Annual Reports by the Conservation Department a tabular record of problems to landowners caused by beaver dam building and tree cutting. We can only speculate here that dynamic changes in the organizational structure and program mission of the Conservation Commission/Department over this time lies at the root cause of this omission.

Although the NY Bureau of Game became a reality in 1931, it pretty much limited its activities to establishing the need for annual beaver trapping seasons authorized by the state legislature in the 1920s. As the 1940s began, game district and statewide tabulations of beaver problems appeared, most likely due to the expansion of the NY Bureau of Game and the creation of an active Furbearer Project, which was assigned the task of keeping track. Except for the war years of 1942, '43 to '45, records of beaver problems acted upon by the Bureau of Game continued until 1960. Again, other priorities established in the 1960s and 1970s by a newly organized NY Bureau of Wildlife prevailed to de-emphasize the need to not only track the number of human conflicts with beavers, but to take little interest in actually managing the annual trapping season until the early 1980s.

The mid to late 1970s could be described as the renaissance for interest in managing furbearing mammals in New York. A turnover of the old guard, a resurgence in the worldwide fur market, the introduction of personal computers and the hiring of young staff under the expansion of wildlife programs in the newly formed New York Environmental Conservation Agency led wildlife biologists stationed throughout the state to initiate research and management plans for beavers on their own.

With regard to record keeping, E. Michael Ermer and the lead author working in far western and central NY, respectively, developed database programs (DBase III) for easily entering and retrieving information on beaver problems in their respective regions and wildlife management units during the early 1980s Sharing this information with other biologists expanded the NY Bureau of Wildlife's ability to efficiently issue permits to those aggrieved by beavers and to compile the numbers into an annual regional and statewide report. [60] (Appendix 2) Annual reporting using these simple computer programs was formalized in the 1992 Statewide Beaver Management Plan and continued into the early 21st century. [61] Such a tabulation of problem beaver locations allowed biologists to analyze population changes and set appropriate trapping seasons in the eight WMUs where beaver problems alone would define the unit's objective. [62] Over the course of seven decades, human/wildlife issues with beaver activity went from a statewide average of 220 a year to over 2,000 by the end of the 20th century. (**Figure 37**)

For the most part the number of beaver-human conflicts increased, as the NY Bureau of Wildlife intentionally or otherwise in-

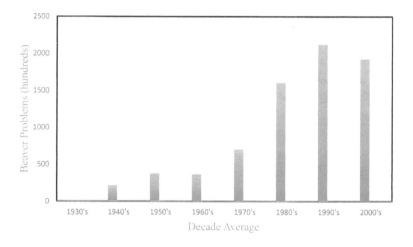

Figure 37. Annual average number of Beaver – Human conflicts in New York (1940's - 2000's)

30th -58th Annual Reports of the NY Conservation Department (1940 – 1968).

1970's - Bishop et.al. 1992, Brown 1979, 1980's – 2000's – Unpublished records NY Bureau of Wildlife, Albany, NY, USA.

creased the beaver population throughout the state in the 1980s. The NY Furbearer Management Team at the time saw the greater good in managing for more active beaver ponds throughout New York, especially where beavers had been suppressed for many decades. This was especially so, because of the wetland/waterfowl benefits provided by beavers clearly enumerated in several New York studies during the 1970s. The issue with beaver-human conflict had always driven the management objectives for this species until biologists finally recognized the benefits that higher beaver populations played in wetland development and management. [63]

The fact that about twelve percent of active beaver colonies create problems for landowners was not seen as a serious impediment to increasing beaver populations. (**Table 6**) Solving human conflict with beaver flooding and tree cutting was seen as economically possible, especially by liberalizing the permitting laws, linking

Table 6. Percent of active beaver colonies that become beaver problems in New York

Year	Number Active Colonies	Number Beaver Problems ***	% Beaver Problems
1993	17,579 *	2,113	11.9
1994	19,350 *	2,404	12.4
1999	17,349 **	2,125	12.2
2000	15,853 **	2,156	13.6
2001	17,386 **	1,708	9.8
2002	17,103 **	1,920	11.2
Total	104,620	12,426	11.9

* *Gordon Batcheller 1995. The 1995 Update on New York State Beaver Management Program.*
NYS DEC, Bureau of Wildlife, Publication, Albany, NY, USA.
** *Robert F. Gotie 2004. Statewide Beaver Data Summary. Unpublished Data, NYS DEC.*
Bureau of Wildlife, Region 7, Cortland, NY, USA.
*** *Unpublished Data, NYS DEC, Bureau of Wildlife, Albany, NY, USA.*

known beaver trappers to complainants and complainants to beaver trappers, promotion of licensed animal control operators, providing well written educational materials for both lethal and non-lethal methods of control, dedicating more staff time to annual surveys, pelt sealing, population analysis, research and expansion of legal trapping seasons. [64] [65] [66] [67] [68] All were clearly desired by aggrieved landowners and conveyed to the NY Bureau of Wildlife through the many sociological studies and public meetings conducted in New York by Cornell University and the NY Bureau of Wildlife. Furbearer biologists were confident that effective harvest options and cost-saving control programs could be implemented for maintaining sustainable populations in the wake of declining pelt values, while also relieving landowners of the total burden for control work.

Although landscape scale furbearer trapping had long served the NY Bureau of Wildlife, the biologists of the FMT who produced the first strategic plan for beaver in 1992 recognized that sooner or later trapping alone might not be enough to regulate beaver population size and demography in the state. Appendix 3 in this plan laid out possible alternative approaches for increasing the removal of beaver throughout the state when merely traditional beaver trapping fell short in removing enough beavers each year. [69] A dozen methods were expounded upon, but in the end only the first five were acted upon by the NY Bureau of Wildlife. All five chosen by the leadership were what they estimated to be the most cost-effective alternatives. To some extent they helped with the issue of a growing need to remove more beavers as the last decade of the 20th century came to an end. But in the final analysis, these first five could not compete with the declining value of the dollar and an aging furbearer trapper cadre.

It was in the last year of the 20th century when Cooperative Extension at Cornell University, with the help of the NY Furbearer Management Team, put together an analysis of regional differences in the types of beaver damage complaints during the 1990s. [70] (**Table 7**) Infrastructure, like public roads, private roads, railroads and man-made

Table 7. Types of beaver problems in upstate NY DEC Regions (1990-1997) *

Region	Infrastructure	Residential	Agricultural	Timber	Other	Total Problems	Total
3	53.8%	19.7%	4.7%	11.8%	10.1%	919	7.2%
4	56.1%	16.3%	10.3%	4.0%	13.3%	1570	12.4%
5	64.0%	15.9%	6.0%	7.7%	6.5%	1570	12.4%
6	59.3%	6.7%	12.5%	13.8%	7.7%	5102	40.2%
7	47.1%	19.3%	16.4%	7.6%	9.7%	1509	11.9%
8	43.1%	20.7%	17.4%	5.8%	12.9%	757	6.0%
9	56.6%	14.0%	11.3%	10.5%	7.8%	1253	9.9%
Statewide	56.4%	13.0%	11.5%	10.1%	9.0%	12,680	100%

* Paul G. Jensen, Paul D. Curtis and Robert F. Gotie 1999. Beaver Damage Complaints in New
York. Unpublished Proceedings of the North American Aquatic Furbearer Symposium,
Starksville, Mississippi, USA.

ponds combined, represented the most complaints about beaver damage in New York at the time and was generally high in all regions of the state.

The regions encompassing the Adirondacks, Tug Hill and St. Lawrence Valley where beaver populations are the densest in New York, not surprisingly, recorded the greatest number of infrastructure problems anywhere in the state. The two central New York regions (7 and 8) where active beaver colonies are much fewer had the fewest infrastructure problems. Complaints involving residential property and agricultural land followed, with Region 7 and 8 of central New York hosting the highest percentage of these types of complaints. This part of New York is heavily peopled in the stream and river valleys from the Pennsylvania line to the Lake Ontario shore.

Over the many years the NY Bureau of Game/Wildlife kept records on beaver problems, its furbearer biologists have quietly known that beaver populations play the most significant role in the ebb and flow of human conflict with this species. However, human development that follows the spread of civilization is a considerable contributing factor. The most important observations from this regional analysis revealed that beaver problems vary between different areas of New York. The drivers for these differences are beaver populations and human development. Our good friend (Roger Miner), an outstanding wildlife professional in central New York, was fond of saying after having helped many people resolve a vexing beaver problem, *"If there is only one beaver left in the world, it will ultimately become a problem to someone."*

We were both privileged to be witnesses and players in the beaver war in the St. Lawrence Valley, which, honestly, was caused by leadership failure at both the regional wildlife office in Watertown, NY and the Furbearer Project in Albany, NY during the mid-1980s. As the number of active beaver colonies began to significantly expand, the Regional Wildlife Manager failed to see the short comings of using a relative metric for a population objective. He continued to use a fixed occupation rate in the face of increasing potential beaver habitat sites, rather than measuring the actual number of active beaver colonies and linking this metric to appropriate action. Likewise, the Furbearer Project leader in Albany, NY remained unmovable far too long on calls by the furbearer biologist in the Watertown wildlife office to lengthen the trapping season. He stayed fixed on a stable trapping season, because the relative population measure remained unchanged even with the obvious growth in the number of active colonies. This failure by both wildlife management offices created a perfect storm between people aggrieved by too many beaver ponds and the NY Bureau of Wildlife in the St. Lawrence Valley.

Not until the mid-1990s after the NY Furbearer Management Team constructed a workable statewide management plan did changes begin to take place with appropriate population objectives and actions to end this major conflict with beaver management. We should also point out the potential for beaver populations as high as they were in the St. Lawrence Valley were never possible in most of New York south of the Mohawk Valley and Lake Ontario. However, continued increases in the human use of our landscape will undoubtedly contribute to future expansion of conflict with this remarkable aquatic mammal. Furthermore, changes in the traditional methods used to manage this species will become absolutely necessary in the 21st Century. [71]

References

[1] Gardiner Bump and Arthur Cook 1941. op. cit.

[2] Gardiner Bump 1941. op. cit.

[3] Robert F. Gotie 1984. Beaver Complaints Handling Policy in Region 7. NYS DEC, Bureau of Wildlife, Region 7, W-137-D, Staff Memo 1/18/84, Cortland, NY, USA.

[4] Bradley L. Griffin 1984. Personal Communication. Natural Resource Supervisor, NYS DEC, Region 7, Cortland, NY, USA.

[5] 48th Annual Report of the Conservation Department New York, 1959.

[6] Kenneth S. Roblee and K.W. Johnson 1980 An Assessment of the Beaver Population in Alleghany State Park in Relation to their Habitat for a Six-Year Period. NYS DEC Fed. Aid in Wildlife Restoration, unpublished Final Report, NY Bureau of Wildlife, Region 9, Project W–139–D, Olean, NY, USA.

[7] Mark K. Brown and Dave Kenyon 1985. Results of Tagging Nuisance Beaver from 1975-1984. NYS DEC, Fed. Aid in Wildlife Restoration, unpublished Final Report, NY Bureau of Wildlife, Region 5, Project W-135-D, Warrensburg, NY, USA.

[8] Robert F. Gotie, E. Michael Ermer, Mark K. Brown and Paul G. Bishop 1988. Progress in Beaver Management in New York State. Unpublished manuscript, NYS Bureau of Wildlife, Region 7, Cortland, NY, USA.

[9] 49th Annual Report to the Conservation Department New York, 1960.

[10] Robert F. Gotie 1984. op. cit.

[11] Kenneth F. Wich 1991. Statewide Policy for Handling Beaver Problems. Policy Memo FW 90-1 Director, Division of Fish and Wildlife, NYS DEC, Albany, NY, USA.

[12] Robert F. Gotie 1995. Time Savings on Region 7 Beaver Management Program. Memo to John C. Proud, Regional Wildlife Manager NYS DEC, Bureau of Wildlife, Region 7, Cortland, NY, USA.

[13] Kenneth F. Wich 1987. Sale of Beaver Pelts taken Under Nuisance Permits. Director, NYS DEC, Division of Fish and Wildlife, Policy Memo FW87-1, Albany, NY, USA.

[14] Robert F. Gotie 1995. Handling of Beaver Problems in Region 7. NYS DEC, Bureau of Wildlife, W-137-D, Region 7, Staff Memo, 5/26/95, Cortland, NY, USA.

[15] Robert F. Gotie 1997. Draft Revision of Statewide Beaver Problems Handling Policy. Memo to FMT, NYS DEC, Bureau of Wildlife, (W-137-D), Region 7, Cortland, NY, USA.

[16] Robert F. Gotie 2001. Statewide Policy for Handling Beaver Problems. Memo to Chief Wildlife Biologist, John Major, NYS DEC, Bureau of Wildlife, (W-137-D), Region 7, Cortland, NY, USA.

[17] Gerald A. Barnhart 1997. Permit Requirements and Guidelines in Protected Streams (ECL-15) and Wetlands (ECL-24) for Breach and Removal of Nuisance Beaver Dams. NYS DEC, Director, Division of Fish, Wildlife and Marine, Memo to NYS DEC, Regional Supervisors of Natural Resources, 9/30/1997, Albany, NY, USA.

[18] Paul G. Bishop, Mark K. Brown, Russel Cole, E. Michael Ermer, Robert F. Gotie, Joseph E. Lamendola, Bruce Penrod, Scott Smith and William Sharick 1994. Position Statement of the Furbearer Management Team Regarding Article 24 Permits for Removal of Beaver Dams on Damage Sites. NYS DEC, Furbearer Management Team, Bureau of Wildlife, Albany, NY, USA.

[19] Food Security Act (FSA) of 1985. 16 U.S.C. Section 3801 (a) (20).

[20] P.A. Keddy 2010. Wetland Ecology; Principles and Conservation (2nd Edition), Cambridge University Press, Cambridge, UK.

[21] Robert F. Gotie and Daryl L. Jenks 1984. op. cit.

[22] G. A. Barnhart 1997. op. cit.

[23] Robert F. Gotie 1993. Article 24 Permits at Problem Beaver Locations. Memo to NYS DEC, Bureau of Wildlife Staff, Region 7, (W-137-D), Cortland, NY, USA.

[24] Herbert Gaylord 1971. A Device for Controlling Water Levels of Beaver Ponds. NYS DEC, Bureau of Wildlife, Region 6, (W-136-D), Publication, Watertown, NY, USA.

[25] H. A. Laramie, Jr. 1963. A Device for Control of Problem Beavers. NH Fish and Game Department, Concord, NH, USA.

[26] Kenneth S. Roblee 1984. Use of Corrugated Plastic Drainage Tubing for Controlling Water Levels at Nuisance Beaver Sites. NY Fish & Game Journal 31 (1): 63-80.

[27] Kenneth S. Roblee 1985. Beaver Control Structures. NYS DEC, Bureau of Wildlife, Region 9, (W-139-D), Publication, Olean, NY, USA.

[28] Roger L. Miner 1993. Not Just Another Beaver Pond Leveler. NYS DEC, Bureau of Wildlife, Region 7, (W-137-D), Publication, Cortland, NY, USA.

[29] Robert F. Gotie 1995. Observations on a Clemson Beaver Pond Leveler Installed at Appalachin Marsh. Memo to Beaver Damage Control Team. NYS DEC, Bureau of Wildlife, Region 7, Cortland, NY, USA.

[30] Elizabeth Tracy 2006. Letter to Victory Highway Department Permit Application ID 7-0564-00017/00005, Agency Program Aid, NYS Division of Environmental Permits, Syracuse, NY, USA.

[31] Robert F. Gotie and Martin Ayers 1974. A Survey of Beaver Damage along the Adirondack RR Thendara to Tupper Lake, NY, unpublished report, NYS DEC, Bureau of Wildlife, Region 6, (W-136-D) Watertown, NY, USA.

[32] Dieter Mueller–Schwarz and S. Heckman 1980. The Social Role of Scent Marking in Beaver (Castor Canadensis). Journal Chemical Ecology. 6: 81-95.

[33] Dieter Mueller-Schwarz and B. Stagge 1983. Behavior of Free-Ranging Beaver (Castor Canadensis) ACTA Zool. Fenn. 174:111-113.

[34] Paul G. Jensen, Paul Curtis, David L. Hamelin 1997. Managing Nuisance Beavers along Roadsides. NYS DEC, Fed. Aid in Wildlife Restoration Program, Grant WE-173-G, Published by Cornell Cooperative Extension.

[35] Paul G. Jensen, Paul D. Curtis, Mark E. Lehnert and David L. Hamelin 2001. Habitat and Structural Factors Influencing Beaver Interference with Highway Culverts. Wildlife Society Bulletin Vol. 29 (2) pp. 654-664.

[36]. Ken G. Purdy, Daniel J. Decker, Richard A. Malecki and John C. Proud 1985. Landowner Tolerance of Beavers; Implications for Damage Management and Control. 2nd Eastern Wildlife Damage Control Conference. pp.83-88.

[37] Jody W. Enck, Ken G. Purdy and Daniel J. Decker 1988. Public Acceptance of Beavers and Beaver Damage in WMU 14 in Region 4. HDRU Series Publ. 88-1. Cornell U. 46 pp.

[38] William F. Siemer and Tommy L. Brown 2003. Attitudes Toward Beaver and Beaver Management: Results from Baseline Studies in New York and Massachusetts. HDRU Series Publication 03-02, Cornell U. 7pp.

[39] Jody W. Enck, Paul G. Bishop, Tommy L. Brown and Joseph E. Lamendola 1992. Beaver-Related Attitudes, Experiences and Knowledge of Key Stakeholders in Wildlife Management Unit 21. HDRU Series No. 92-7, Cornell U. 74 pp.

[40] Thomas Payne 1776. Common Sense. Printed and sold by R. Bell, Philadelphia, PA, USA

[41] Robert F. Gotie 1995. Active Beaver Colonies/mi² Versus Beaver Problem Locations/mi². NYS DEC, Bureau of Wildlife, Fed. Aid in Wildlife Restoration, unpublished data, Project W-137-D, Cortland, NY, USA.

[42] Michael Runge 1997. op. cit.

[43] Gordon R. Batcheller 1995. The 1995 Update on the NYS Beaver Management Program. NYS DEC, Bureau of Wildlife, Publication, Albany, NY, USA.

[44] Joseph E Lamendola 1996. Region 6 Nuisance Beaver Report 1995. NYS DEC, Bureau of Wildlife, Region 6, Watertown, NY, USA.

[45] Robert F. Gotie 1992. Consequences... The New York Forest Owner, July/August 1992.

[46] Thomas A. Decker, Robert F. Gotie, John F. Organ and Gordon R. Batcheller 1996. Return of Beaver in the Northeastern States – A case Study. Proc. Seminar Tour in Rural Development and Conservation in Africa – Studies in Community Resource Management, USAID.

[47] E. Michael Ermer 1988. Managing Beaver in New York. The Conservationist, March-April:36-39.

[48] Paul G. Bishop, Mark K. Brown, Russel. Cole, E.Michael Ermer, Robert F. Gotie, Joseph E. Lamendola, Bruce Penrod, Scott Smith and William Sharick 1994. Summary of the Public Meetings on Beaver Management in Gouverneur (3/29/94) and Potsdam (3/30/94), NY, NYS DEC, Bureau of Wildlife, Albany, NY, USA.

[49] Robert F. Gotie and Joseph Lamendola 1995. Beaver Management Challenges: Now and in the Future. NY Chapter TWS Annual Conference.

Rochester, NY January 1995.

[50] Robert F. Gotie 1994. Beaver Management in New York. A Slide Talk Given at Public Meetings in St. Lawrence Co, Gouverneur and Potsdam, NY, NYS DEC Bureau of Wildlife, Region 7, Cortland, NY, USA.

[51] Robert F. Gotie and John C. Proud 1993. NY Bureau of Wildlife, Region 7, Beaver Management in New York. Presentation given at Onondaga County Audubon Society, Syracuse, NY, USA.

[52] Dave Hamlin, Dan Dougherty, Greg Fuerst, Daryl Jenks, Tom Raffaldi, Vance Gilligan, Gary Golja and Ben Tuller 1997. Beaver Damage Control Techniques Manual. NYS DEC, Bureau of Wildlife Publication, Albany, NY, USA, 40pp.

[53] John C. Proud 1986. Landowner Assistance – Beaver Damage Complaints. Memo to NYS DEC Regional Wildlife Managers, NYS DEC, Bureau of Wildlife, Region7, Cortland, NY, USA.

[54] Kenneth F. Wich 1983. Nuisance Wildlife Control License. Statewide Policy Memo FW-83-2, 3/30/1983, NYS DEC, Director, Division of Fish and Wildlife, Albany, NY, USA.

[55] McKinney's Consolidated Laws of New York Annotated. Environmental Conservation Law Chapter 45-B of the Consolidated Laws. Article 11 Fish and Wildlife, Title 11, Trapping, 018.

[56] Mark K. Brown, E. Michael Ermer, Robert F. Gotie, Joseph E. Lamendola, Bruce Penrod, William Sharick and Scott Smith. 2002. Snares and Snaring for Capturing Nuisance Beaver. NYS DEC, Bureau of Wildlife, Fur Management Team. Publication, Albany, NY 2/11/2002.

[57] Robert F. Gotie 2003. Recommendation – Nuisance Wildlife Program. Memo to Bureau of Wildlife Management Team. 1/16/2003. NYS Furbearer Management Team, NY Bureau of Wildlife, Region 7, Cortland, NY, USA.

[58] John Major 2003. Recommendation for the Nuisance Wildlife Program. Memo to Furbearer Management Team. 2/11/2003. Chief Wildlife Biologist, NY Bureau of Wildlife, Management Team, NYS Division of Fish, Wildlife and Marine, Albany, NY, USA.

[59] 9th Annual Report 1919. op. cit.

[60] John C. Proud 1986. op. cit.

[61] Robert F. Gotie 2001. op. cit.

[62] Paul G. Bishop et.al. 1992. op. cit.

[63] Gardiner Bump and Arthur Cook 1941. op. cit.

[64] Joseph L. Lamendola 2001. Standard Activity Permit for Highway Departments in St. Lawrence County. Re: Beaver Problems with Roads. Operating Policy, NYS DEC, NY Bureau of Wildlife, Region 6, Watertown, NY, USA.

[65] Robert F. Gotie 2003. op. cit.

[66] Paul G. Bishop et. al. 1994. op. cit.

[67] Paul D. Curtis, J. Montan, R. Dennis Faulknham and Joseph L. Lamendola 1994. Beaver Management Working Group; St. Lawrence County. NYS DEC, Bureau of Wildlife, Region 6, Watertown, NY, USA.

[68] Jody W. Enck, Paul G. Bishop, Tommy L. Brown and Joseph L. Lamendola 1992. Beaver Related Attitudes, Experiences and Knowledge of Key Stakeholders in Wildlife management Unit 21. HDRU Series No. 92-7, Cornell U. 74pp.

[69] Paul G. Bishop et.al. 1992. op. cit.

[70] Paul G. Jensen, Paul D. Curtis and Robert F. Gotie 1999. Regional analysis of beaver damage complaints in New York. Unpublished Proceedings of the North American Aquatic Furbearer Symposium, Starkville, MS, USA.

[71] Thomas A. Decker and Gordon R. Batcheller 1993. Furbearer Management in Transition: Challenges for the future. Northeast Wildlife 50:153-157.

CHAPTER VI

ANIMAL RIGHTS ACTIVISM

New York State, during the last quarter of the 20th century, was a hot bed of animal rights activism. The continued use of the steel jaw foot trap and the killing of wild animals, whether closely regulated and monitored or not, was seen as evil and inhumane by a large segment of New York's citizens. This situation as we know it now was merely a reflection of the fact that more than half of New York's population lives in the greater NY Metro area where an actual interaction with wildlife of any type is remote. In upstate New York most of the people residing here, even in the cities, frequently interact positively or negatively with wildlife such as beavers. Here, questions about humanness and animal rights were much less prevalent. For the most part, New York residents upstate are far more pragmatic.

Issues raised by animal rights activists ranged from outright bans of trapping in single townships, or better yet in the entire state, to prohibiting the use of steel traps, to the righteousness of killing wildlife for sport, food or monetary value. Animal activists even challenged the state's policy on handling problem beavers, demanding it not make it easier to issue permits under the two laws specifically designed decades ago to help people aggrieved by beavers damaging their property. [1] [2] Pond levelers, bafflers and every other non-lethal means of saving a problem beaver site were offered as an alternative. [3]

At this time nearly all of the state's wildlife professional and technical personnel were versed in the game management principles of sustained use expressed by Aldo Leopold, the father of modern wildlife management. [4] Most had years of experience with issues involving trapping, hunting, fishing and handling problems confronting people and wildlife. Most had extensive experience with water level controllers, and most of the wildlife field staff had serious doubts as to their overall efficacy. Both authors experienced washed out roads, small man-made ponds and large beaver flows where pond levelers were used, but neglected, and eventually failed. [5] [6] To the furbearer biologists in New York, this was a very real obstacle. Without constant maintenance pond levelers fail, because most people with a beaver problem have little interest in constructing, installing and regularly maintaining these devices, unless someone else is willing to assume the maintenance costs themselves.

The concern of animal rights and welfare groups was not only restricted to the United States. The European Economic Community (EEC), which later became the European Union (EU) during the early 1990s, also became vested in the animal rights movement of the times. This multi-country community of individual governments in Europe debated a trade import ban on wild furs exported from the major fur producing countries like the U.S., Canada and Russia that used traps that they considered inhumane. [7] The European Union (EU) was a significant market for wild furs coming from New York and other states. Hence, natural resource agencies in the U.S. became justifiably concerned about its impact on their furbearer management programs, especially the American beaver, a well-known problem species. [8]

In 1993 the co-author, in an address to the Northeast Fur Resources Technical Committee about the EU fur import ban, described the current situation with beaver populations in New York. At this time there were 17,648 active colonies that produced 2,113 damage locations at an estimated cost to landowners and highway departments a total of $5.5 million. A stronger worldwide fur market during the 1993-94 beaver trapping season generated a 56% increase in beavers harvested over the previous season and helped to slow the growth in the number of active colonies entering the 1994–95 season. [9] Nonetheless, New York's beavers still exceeded the expressed goal of 14,000 active colonies in the Fall of 1994. Fearing this trade ban, New York's furbearer biologists, with input from three other NY DEC Divisions and the Natural Heritage Program, completed an assessment of the possible consequences of losing the ability to control beaver populations by the year 2000. What they found did not bode well for New Yorkers nor the New York landscape and the stream trout fishery. [10] To prevent such a tragedy in New York and elsewhere, biologists joined a multi-state effort with Canada to meet the requirements of the EU humane trapping regulations. [11] The NY Bureau of Wildlife had earlier suggested other methods of increasing the harvest of beaver, such as a hunting season, exclusive territory trapping, state per pelt subsidies and trapper cooperatives. None gained traction except for longer beaver trapping seasons.

To further address the many issues raised by animal rights activists in New York, over the years several articles, handouts and booklets on the status of furbearers and trapping laws and regulations were written beginning in the 1970s and provided to New York legislators and the general public. [12] [13] [14] New York's goal was to educate the citizens of New York about traps and trapping of furbearers in the state. Many hours were spent during the last decades of the 20th century by biologists testifying before New York's Environmental Conservation Legislative Committee or writing letters to New Yorkers addressing their concerns. Staff of the NY Bureau of Wildlife also partnered with the New York State Trappers Association in the 1980s to examine the trapping systems used in New York and offer improved methods to New York trappers. [15] This partnership continued well into the 21st century.

In 1980 the NY Division of Fish and Wildlife developed and then implemented with the assistance of the NY Trapper's Association a mandatory trapper education program for new trappers. [16] Many field biologists and technicians throughout New York became instructors along with veteran trappers to man the Trapper Training Courses. New York biologists, in the 1970s through the 1990s, also took an active role in the national effort of trap testing research, mainly to address animal welfare, efficiency and selectivity of currently used traps. [17] [18] [19] It became crystal clear in the early 1990s that trappers, natural resource agencies and the wild fur market were in for significant changes, if the world-wide tradition of fur harvesting were to continue into the 21st century. [20]

A booklet entitled *Best Management Practices for Trapping Beaver in the United States*, published by the Association of Fish and Wildlife Agencies, contained the findings and recommendations of New York's 20th century research on selectivity with the 10"x10' rotating jaw beaver/otter trap. [21] [22] By the end of the 1990s, the wildlife biologists of the state committed themselves to *"finding a better mouse trap"* that would promote the traditions of furbearer trapping and the humane treatment of furbearing mammals well into the 21st century. [23] [24]

References

[1] Michael Hill 1996. NY Wants to Make it Easier to Kill Nuisance Beaver. Auburn Citizen, 4/28/96.

[2] Joseph E. Lamendola 2001. Standard Activity Permit for Highway Departments in St. Lawrence Co. re: Beaver Problems with Roads, NYS DEC, Bureau of Wildlife, Region 6 Watertown, NY, USA.

[3] Sharon Brown 1995. Friends of Beaversprite. Letter to Eric Fried, Leader Wildlife Management Section, NYS DEC, Bureau of Wildlife, Delmar, NY, USA.

[4] Aldo Leopold 1933. Game Management. New York: Scribner's.

[5] Robert F. Gotie 1988. Field Investigation – Washout of Spaulsbury Road, Town of Amboy, Oswego County. Memo to J.C. Proud, Regional Wildlife Manager, NYS DEC, Bureau of Wildlife, Region 7, Cortland, NY, USA.

[6] J.R. Clairborne and Franklin Crawford 1997. Beaver Dam, Heavy Rains Wash Away Track. Ithaca Journal, 11/4/97

[7] J. Michael Kelly 1993. Is Trapping on its' Last Legs? Syracuse Post Standard, 12/23/93.

[8] Robert F. Gotie 1992. Synopsis of the June 1992 meeting of the Fur Insti-

tute of Canada: Wild Fur and the International Market, Quebec City, Quebec, Memo to J. C. Proud, Regional Wildlife Manager, NY Bureau of Wildlife, Region 7, Cortland, NY, and Gordon Batcheller, Fur Project Leader, Albany, NY, USA.

[9] Mark K. Brown 1994. Economic profile of the US Fur Industry – Update on New York's Beaver Management Program. Northeast Fur Resources Technical Committee Meeting, Chittenden, VT, USA.

[10] Paul G. Bishop et. al. 1994. op. cit.

[11] Glenn R. Delaney 1994. Meeting by Senator Breaux with Ambassador Mickey Cantor on the EU Fur Ban. Memo to Chief Wildlife Biologist, Gary Parsons, NYS DEC, Bureau of Wildlife from Gordon Batcheller, Fur Project Leader, Albany, NY, USA.

[12] Anonymous 1977. Trapping – New York Wildlife. NYS DEC, FW- P105 (9/77).

[13] Mark Brown, Gary Parsons and Bruce Penrod 1980. About Furbearers and Trapping in New York. NYS DEC, Bureau of Wildlife, Publication, Albany, NY, USA.

[14] Gary R. Parsons 1977. The Case for Trapping. The Conservationist, Sept-Oct.

[15] Gordon Batcheller 1989. NYS DEC – NYSTA Joint Trapping Initiative. NYS DEC Publiccation.

[16] Ronald Howard, Louis Berchielli, Gary Parsons and Mark Brown 1980. Trapping Furbearers – Student Manual, NYS Department of Environmental Conservation, Division of Fish and Wildlife, Albany, NY, USA.

[17] Anonymous 2016. Best Management Practices for Trapping Beaver in the United States. International Association of Fish & Wildlife Agencies, Publication, USA.

[18] Louis Berchelli, Jr. and Benjamin Tullar 1980. op. cit.

[19] Benjamin F. Tullar, Jr 1984. Evaluation of Leg-hold Trap for Capturing Foxes and Raccoons. NY Fish & Game Journal 31:(1)97-107.

[20] Robert F. Gotie 1992. Changing Times and Difficult Choices. NYS DEC, Division of Fish, Wildlife and Marine, Furbearer Management Newsletter, Albany, NY, USA.

[21] Robert F. Gotie, Marie Kautz, Mark K. Brown and Edward Kautz 2000. Selectivity with #330™ Conibears. The Trapper and Predator Caller Magazine, October 2000.

[22] I.A.F.W.A. 2003. Best Management Practices for Trapping Coyotes in the Eastern US. 16 pp.

[23] Angie Berchielli 1998. Trapping in the 21st Century. NYS Trappers Association, Ilion, NY, USA.

[24] Robert F. Gotie and Marie Kautz 2000. Finding a Better Mouse Trap. NYS Division of Fish Wildlife and Marine, Furbearer Management Newsletter, Winter 2000.

AFTERWORD

We started this historical narrative with the following words written in 1987, *"the status of beavers in New York has changed many times in the last three centuries, as have people's attitudes towards the American Beaver. Whether the positive or negative value of beavers has always been fully understood is still unclear today.*

"As the 21ˢᵗ Century moves forward, the chapters that follow will describe the steps taken to purposely return and eventually increase the American Beaver from none to many during the 20ᵗʰ Century in New York State. It is however likely, the management philosophy that prevailed during this century will not survive the next generation of management thought, just as the 18ᵗʰ and 19ᵗʰ Century viewpoint was swept aside in the 1890's."

These prophetic words could not be any clearer today after nearly two decades into the 21ˢᵗ century. The late 20ᵗʰ century NY Bureau of Wildlife placed a premium on managing beaver populations to produce a significant increase in waterfowl-wetland benefits in NY. In a personal interview with the current NY Furbearer Management Team, early 21ˢᵗ century beaver management philosophy now focuses solely on reducing beaver-human conflict. Little accurate empirical data is collected each year on population size or the number of beavers removed by trapping in the wildlife management units, originally developed from the ecological subdivision of the state.

Annual trapping seasons that once recognized the difference in population potential throughout New York had been reduced to only four Wildlife Management Units by the year 2020, and haven't been changed in at least a decade. No specific and measurable population objectives are defined, nor are there measurable objectives for an acceptable number of human beaver conflicts. No emphasis is placed on using the beaver's pond building behavior to create small wetlands. Only the *"squawk index,"* coined by the late William Severinghaus, is used today to evoke changes in legal trapping seasons. The only item remaining from the original management plan from the 1980s and 1990s is the ease with which a person complaining about an issue with beavers can obtain permission to kill them.

There is no one reason nor person to blame here. Several modern-day factors have caused this shift once again in how the NY Bureau of Wildlife manages a keystone species. More priority is placed on expanding the distribution and harvest of the uncommon furbearers (fisher, otter, bobcat, marten). The continuing decline in the dollar value of beaver pelts, as well as an aging cadre of active trappers with low recruitment of younger people into the ranks, has reduced the overall number of participating trappers willing to take significant numbers of beavers. Few biologists and technicians are willing to risk their life and overcome air sickness in small aircraft, nor has any effort been spent on drone technology or satellite imagery to survey the extent of beaver activity. Furthermore, these factors and tighter budgets in an era of ever-increasing responsibility towards other environmental priorities have combined to press for de-empathizing the management of New York's most important furbearing mammal. New York now joins many other states with a similar hands-off management strategy. Whether New York will blindly follow California, its sister liberal state on the opposite side of the country, in a complete prohibition of furbearer trapping in the 21st century, only time will tell.

In the progression of Wildlife Management Science, this contemporary change in NY beaver management philosophy essentially turns the clock back seven decades to a time when managing all furbearing mammals was at its lowest ebb. We recognize that change accompanies every generation and we are certain that changes will again be made as the 21st century marches on. Nonetheless, as two of the earliest and original architects of intensively managing beaver populations for the benefits they provide to wetland wildlife diversity, we can only feel great regret at this current evolution. For us and the other members of the original NY Furbearer Management Team we were honored to have played a significant role in elevating the status of the American beaver in New York State during the 20th Century.

ACKNOWLEDGEMENTS

Several New Yorkers were instrumental in bringing the American Beaver back from the abyss and ultimately elevating its status from vertebrate pest to valuable natural resource in the 20th century. The following made significant early contributions to beaver management in New York. For his influential work on behalf of beavers in the early years, thanks and gratitude go to Harry V. Radford. Without his abiding interest and tenacious political clout, we may not have returned beaver to prominence so soon in New York. Charles E. Johnson's report on the "Adirondack Beaver" led to an accurate accounting of the beaver harvest through a requirement for trappers to have their pelts officially tagged by a state agency representative. This system of accounting for the annual beaver harvest lasted nearly 75 years. Arthur Cook and Gardiner Bump were the first to recognize the important benefits besides pelt value of this keystone species in the 1930s and 1940s. It was they who also acknowledged the vast differences in habitat suitably and then established the first rudimentary population objectives for this species throughout the state.

During the 1960s and 1970s, it was Gary Parsons and Nathaniel Dickinson's sincere belief more could be done to directly manage beavers for the benefits that Art Cook and Gardiner Bump identified years earlier. Their steadfast conviction renewed the NY Bureau of Wildlife's interest for managing this species and inspired the next generation of wildlife biologists to actually develop a complete action plan for treating beavers as an asset rather than a liability.

We would be remiss to not acknowledge the contributions by Scott R. Smith, Joseph E. Lamendola,

E. Michael Ermer, Paul G. Bishop, Bruce Penrod, Thomas Sutter, Russel Cole and Arthur Jacobsen whose dedicated work on the essential elements of beaver population management in upstate New York made it possible to achieve a milestone in the annals of wildlife management. We will always be grateful to the other biologists, technicians, Conservation officers and office staff who handled thousands of beaver damage complaints, placed seals on greasy beaver pelts, flew in cramped light aircraft under dangerous conditions to count active beaver ponds and lastly kept mundane records and prepared annual reports.

The last of this historical narrative was written as an afterword and is based upon interviews with current NY Furbearer Team members: Scott R. Smith, Michael Putnam, William Scharra, Tim Pryszczynski and Tim Watson and others. Without the assistance and inspiration from all of these former and current biologists, this manuscript could not have been written. Many thanks to Michael Cavanaugh of Slingerlands, NY and Brian and Barbara Dam of Vernon Center, NY for editing the manuscript and making it a more readable narrative.

BIOGRAPHICAL SKETCH
OF AUTHORS

Robert F. Gotie

Retired as a Senior Wildlife Biologist in 2005, with the New York State Department of Environmental Conservation, Bureau of Wildlife, Region 7, Cortland, NY, after a 34-year career that began as a Biologist Aide in the summers of 1968 and 1970. He holds a BS degree (1969) in Wildlife Science from Cornell University and an MS degree (1972) in Wildlife Science from Texas A&M University, where he was a Wildlife Research Assistant with the Texas Agricultural Experiment Station from Sept. 1970 to Sept. 1972. Between 1970 and 2005 he worked tirelessly on a variety of wildlife management issues in Texas and New York, nearly losing his life in a plane crash while conducting aerial beaver surveys in 1990. He has authored or co-authored many published technical and popular articles, as well as countless Federal Aid in Wildlife Restoration Reports, on topics ranging from the esoteric to the pragmatic in wildlife management science. He led the effort in the 1970s to establish a statewide telephone survey of trappers and small game hunters that lasted 20 years. He played a major role in writing New York's first beaver management plan in 1992. He was the principal architect of New York's Citizen Task Force Project on deer management in 1990 and the #330 Conibear™ beaver trap study in 1998. He was a foremost co-leader of New York's River otter restoration project in Central & Western NY between 1995 and 2001. Between 1998 and 2003 he led the statewide Furbearer Management Team. He is a duly elected member of the Beta Rho chapter of Phi Sigma Society (1972), a society dedicated to research in the Biological Sciences. He has been a member of both the National and NY State Chapter of The Wildlife Society since 1968. He is a life member of the National Eagle Scout Association, and as a Board member of the American Wildlife Conservation Foundation, he chairs the AWCF Grants Committee. Daughter Jennifer is an active-duty Lt. Colonel now serving with the US Army's ROTC Program, Syracuse, NY. Son, R. Christian is a mechanical engineer and manager of R&D at Dillon Aero, Scottsdale, AZ. Robert and wife Mary Ann reside in Truxton, NY where they have both been actively involved in the civic life of this small rural community, the Boy and Girl Scouts of Cortland County, the Cortland Rotary Club, Catholic Charities of Cortland and St Patrick's Catholic Church.

Mark K. Brown

Retired in 2003 after working as a Senior Wildlife Biologist for 31 years with the New York State Department of Environmental Conservation, Bureau of Wildlife, Region 5, Warrensburg, NY. He holds a BS degree in Wildlife Management from the University of Vermont (1972). He began working summers in High School for the New York State Conservation Department, Division of Lands and Forests. In college he worked for the Lake George Park Commission (Law Enforcement Officer) and NYSDEC Bureau of Fisheries as a Biologist Aide. He began his career as a wildlife biologist with the NYS DEC, Bureau of Wildlife in 1973. He was actively involved in research and management on such species as deer, bear, moose, turkey, waterfowl, birds, endangered species, reptiles and amphibians. However, he is best known for his work with furbearers. With fellow Biologists from other DEC Regions in New York, they accomplished numerous research studies, surveys and harvest management projects on fisher, marten, beaver, otter, bobcat, mink and coyote. He has authored or co-authored over 75 technical papers, articles, final reports and abstracts on furbearer management. He was especially active during his career with several translocation projects of furbearers including a fisher project in the Catskills Mountains of NY (1970's), a fisher relocation project in northern Pennsylvania (1990's), a marten project in the Green Mountains of VT (1990's), an otter project in Central and Western New York (1990's), and a lynx recovery project in the Adi-

rondack Mountains of New York. Along with fellow Biologists Gary Parsons and Gary Will, he organized the initial beginnings of the Northeast Fur Resources Technical Committee, which was comprised of furbearer biologist from North Carolina to Newfoundland. He is a highly sought-after speaker, having given over 725 presentations on various fish and wildlife topics to numerous groups ranging from elementary students to sportsmen's clubs to college wildlife classes. He is a board member of the American Wildlife Conservation Foundation, active member of the Warren County Soil and Water Board, the Warrensburg Historical Society, 4H Shooting Sports program, and is a NYSDEC hunter and trapper education instructor. He and his wife Charlise live in Warrensburg, NY where they own and manage Brown's Tree Farm. They have four children: Shana graduated from the University of Maine, MS SUNY Albany and works in Asheville, NC as a Clinical Physiologist, Trevor graduated from the University of Connecticut and works for the Florida Fish and Wildlife Commission, Seth works for the US Forest Service in California and Jenifer graduated from the University of Pittsburgh and works as a Registered Nurse in the Labor and Delivery Unit at Glens Falls Hospital, Glens Falls, NY.

APPENDIX I

BEAVER HARVEST BY COUNTY (1934-2010)

County	1934	1935	1936	1937	1938	1939	1940	1941	1942	1943	1944
Albany			No Season			No Season	No Season				36
Allegany			"			"	"	61			70
Broome			"			"	"				
Cattaraugus			"			"	"	124	156		234
Cayuga			"			"	"				
Chautauqua			"			"	"	204	205		
Chemung			"			"	"		22		20
Chenango			"			"	"				
Clinton	76	56	"	22	49	"	"	99	118	79	105
Columbia			"			"	"		66		
Cortland			"			"	"				
Delaware			"			"	"				
Dutchess			"			"	"		39		
Erie			"			"	"				
Essex	452	363	"	384	418	"	"	347	415	232	288
Franklin	441	393	"	268	392	"	"	371	476	315	384
Fulton			"			"	"	151	174	109	131
Genesee			"			"	"				
Greene			"			"	"				
Hamilton	1,071	551	"	537	645	"	"	657	829	444	587
Herkimer	612	163	"	191	318	"	"	288	243	134	242
Jefferson			"			"	"				
Lewis	214	136	"	71	159	"	"		178	105	140
Livingston			"			"	"				
Madison			"			"	"				
Monroe			"			"	"				
Montgomery			"			"	"	1			
Niagara			"			"	"				
Oneida	52	36	"	31	36	"	"		73		60
Onondaga			"			"	"				
Ontario			"			"	"				
Orange	214	124	"	86	86	"	"	87	113	52	64
Orleans			"			"	"				
Oswego			"			"	"		70		48
Otsego			"			"	"				
Putnam			"	11	9	"	"	17			
Rensselaer			"			"	"	89	148	100	107
Rockland	163	147	"	50	68	"	"	44	82		
Saratoga			"			"	"	62	89	33	21
Schenectady			"			"	"				
Schoharie			"			"	"				
Schuyler			"			"	"				46
Seneca			"			"	"				
St. Lawrence	326	285	"	180	347	"	"	284	341	301	317
Steuben			"			"	"				113
Sullivan	313	244	"	93		"	"		63	135	61
Tioga			"			"	"				
Tompkins			"			"	"				
Ulster			"			"	"				
Warren			"	90	112	"	"	146	175	113	
Washington			"			"	"	17			
Wayne			"			"	"				
Westchester			"			"	"	6			
Wyoming			"			"	"				
Yates			"			"	"				34
Statewide	3,934	2,498	"	2,014	2,639	"	"	3,055	4,075	2,152	3,138

Appendix 1. NY Trapper Harvest of Beavers by County.

County	1945	1946	1947	1948	1949	1950	1951	1952	1953	1954	1955	1956
Albany		63			30	7		74		67	NDA	NDA
Allegany		56		38				89	125	84	"	"
Broome				35		25	58	43	50	19	"	"
Cattaraugus		249		204		158	175	94	190	131	"	"
Cayuga						10		22	5	3	"	"
Chautauqua		407		344		258	327	150	343	185	"	"
Chemung		31		37		29	1	18	32		"	"
Chenango				59		36	50	155	63	53	"	"
Clinton	146	168			71	123	243	186	259	154	"	"
Columbia								22	1		"	"
Cortland				45		18	25	49	19		"	"
Delaware								7	42	28	"	"
Dutchess		45			44	19		12	56		"	"
Erie		6				18			39	15	"	"
Essex	355	359		327	81	132	279	299	572	303	"	"
Franklin	679	675		844	239	358	723	1,164	1,619	351	"	"
Fulton	140	102				56	178	124	199	117	"	"
Genesee		7							28	9	"	"
Greene						13		105	74	53	"	"
Hamilton	702	764		593	310	318	775	688	1,218	1,005	"	"
Herkimer	345	430		356	107	178	379	402	743	593	"	"
Jefferson					165		509	199			"	"
Lewis		350			159	184	362	226	619	607	"	"
Livingston						3	14		30	5	"	"
Madison						33	34	84	98	43	"	"
Monroe											"	"
Montgomery											"	"
Niagara											"	"
Oneida	122	111				60	108	39	85	67	"	"
Onondaga						8	10	27	15	5	"	"
Ontario		6				8	16		43	11	"	"
Orange		62			67			43	115		"	"
Orleans										12	"	"
Oswego	84	52				54	103	46	72	45	"	"
Otsego						50		126	53	44	"	"
Putnam		36			24	12		19	65		"	"
Rensselaer		51			48		92	52		49	"	"
Rockland		31			19				19		"	"
Saratoga		146			54	52	130	107	158	75	"	"
Schenectady								4			"	"
Schoharie						21		50	35	19	"	"
Schuyler		25		48		24	35	16	40		"	"
Seneca		1									"	"
St. Lawrence	635	642		1,038	383	406	873	1,254	1,281	957	"	"
Steuben		125		125		65	126	68	132	101	"	"
Sullivan						44		302		206	"	"
Tioga		32		66		19	11	21	48		"	"
Tompkins		53		28		10	31	10	41		"	"
Ulster		56				36		41	89		"	"
Warren		357			134	130	262	233	320	211	"	"
Washington				111	23	17	52	45	70	22	"	"
Wayne									6	4	"	"
Westchester					8	1		1			"	"
Wyoming	67	51				23			61	31	"	"
Yates		18		30		18	21	15	22	22	"	"
Statewide	3,275	5,567		4,328	1,966	3,034	6,002	6,731	9,194	5,826	"	"

County	1957	1958	1959	1960	1961	1962	1963	1964	1965	1966*	1967
Albany	49	16	35	20	No	Pelt	Tagging	By	ECO's	24	13
Allegany	89	775	82	143	"	"	"	"	"	190	144
Broome	82	43	67	129	"	"	"	"	"		60
Cattaraugus	109	82	185	188	"	"	"	"	"	148	142
Cayuga	2	9	12	25	"	"	"	"	"		20
Chautauqua	219		171	194	"	"	"	"	"	385	167
Chemung	28	37		45	"	"	"	"	"	27	22
Chenango	66	52	82	129	"	"	"	"	"		172
Clinton	32	198	268	382	"	"	"	"	"	35	61
Columbia	5	3	10	10	"	"	"	"	"	8	
Cortland	22	15		51	"	"	"	"	"		55
Delaware	61	40	78	114	"	"	"	"	"	92	85
Dutchess	57	42	32	16	"	"	"	"	"		11
Erie	32	3	5	3	"	"	"	"	"		10
Essex	253	437	382	406	"	"	"	"	"	240	221
Franklin	490	803	633	802	"	"	"	"	"	104	249
Fulton	216	282	193	94	"	"	"	"	"	110	63
Genesee	19				"	"	"	"	"		6
Greene	80	51	94	91	"	"	"	"	"	51	53
Hamilton	715	658	447	1,180	"	"	"	"	"	725	516
Herkimer	610	743	363	649	"	"	"	"	"	10	540
Jefferson	180	139	169	48	"	"	"	"	"		106
Lewis	627	875	464	1,185	"	"	"	"	"		547
Livingston	10	4	3	30	"	"	"	"	"		15
Madison	59	51	88	144	"	"	"	"	"		34
Monroe	2		4	2	"	"	"	"	"		
Montgomery	1		10	5	"	"	"	"	"	2	4
Niagara					"	"	"	"	"		
Oneida	147	129	69	238	"	"	"	"	"		64
Onondaga	9	38	36	100	"	"	"	"	"		42
Ontario	19	10	30	29	"	"	"	"	"		40
Orange	94	13	36	57	"	"	"	"	"		1
Orleans	10		3		"	"	"	"	"		
Oswego	105	140	67	136	"	"	"	"	"		153
Otsego	132	124	184	133	"	"	"	"	"	71	87
Putnam	7		1		"	"	"	"	"		
Rensselaer	44	39	32	35	"	"	"	"	"	11	24
Rockland					"	"	"	"	"		
Saratoga	148	96	98	80	"	"	"	"	"	56	82
Schenectady	5	5	13	2	"	"	"	"	"	3	
Schoharie	47	16	37	66	"	"	"	"	"	51	35
Schuyler	19	17		32	"	"	"	"	"	27	38
Seneca	1	1	1		"	"	"	"	"		
St. Lawrence	1,73	1,218	945	1,697	"	"	"	"	"	17	698
Steuben	60	49	97	110	"	"	"	"	"	156	109
Sullivan	129	158	202	255	"	"	"	"	"		124
Tioga	32	19		34	"	"	"	"	"		24
Tompkins	18	15		18	"	"	"	"	"		1
Ulster	206	60	84	45	"	"	"	"	"	6	45
Warren	213	141	166	179	"	"	"	"	"	64	138
Washington	41	70	44	43	"	"	"	"	"	9	16
Wayne	6	14	7	15	"	"	"	"	"		16
Westchester					"	"	"	"	"		
Wyoming	53			1	"	"	"	"	"		38
Yates	35	24	18	39	"	"	"	"	"		19
Statewide	6,768	7,056	6,047	9,429	"	"	"	"	"	2,622	5,110

Appendix 1. NY Trapper Harvest of Beavers by County (Continued)

*Pelt tagging not required for 33 counties

County	1968	1969	1970	1971	1972	1973	1974	1975	1976	1977	1978	1979
Albany	38	21	27	14	51	84	25	39	39	69	71	67
Allegany	156	218	196	140	172	413	162	87				
Broome	74	86	96	11	68	299	111	59	65	72	41	79
Cattaraugus	120	188	178	158	144	306	337	171	290	282		
Cayuga	23	36	16	14	41	94	66	55	47	53	44	47
Chautauqua	132	170	200	135	138	404	253	143	211	168		
Chemung	23	39	21	28	11	63	49	36	23	34	7	42
Chenango	84	137	110	2	96	167	109	60	97	73	34	94
Clinton	179	54	119			571	348	404	571	592	435	706
Columbia	1	1	9		27	16	2	23	30	43	42	37
Cortland	40	33	52		55	59	58	51	27	57	24	8
Delaware	130	115	128	130	203	784	170	177	124	180	165	352
Dutchess		7	19	5	23	27	31	67	27	72	83	64
Erie	11	10	14	18	23	36	15	17	30	16		
Essex	408	254	370	116	168	740	352	397	476	442	244	499
Franklin	472	325	434	207	395	957	565	746	924	1,126	683	1,060
Fulton	90	7	3		11	308	278	219	222	336	202	287
Genesee	5	18	12	20		2	4			8	6	
Greene	45	34	22	21	74	157	85	63	52	85	94	136
Hamilton	980	745	504	371	928	1,090	908	687	771	852	502	729
Herkimer	591	627	419	75	203	530	526	603	545	758	421	551
Jefferson	240	268	181	103	283	693	319	312	488	824	386	972
Lewis	711	666	145	201	503	1,146	531	640	1,063	1,299	647	1,258
Livingston	10	30	17	16	8	54	28	34	14	32	6	3
Madison	44	45	38		35	149	85	49	69	66	35	22
Monroe	3	4	6	4	7	7	4		3	12	2	2
Montgomery	3		1		8	27	28	30	35	71	42	63
Niagara		5	6	3				7				
Oneida	105	92	34	47	91	182	103	135	224	203	169	219
Onondaga	8	44	29		50	71	63	68	39	22	12	22
Ontario	25	28	22	10	12	36	38	16	45	49	18	16
Orange	35	18	32	19	47	57	36	35	31	68	26	40
Orleans	5	6	16		9	2	2		11	9	3	4
Oswego	189	149	137	121	202	233	63	177	332	268	192	402
Otsego	230	177	57	78	99	189	111	110	132	189	212	233
Putnam	1		4		4		1	9		3		1
Rensselaer	11		22	4	34	19	12	35	40	59	79	64
Rockland		1	2			17	2	1	1	5		2
Saratoga	114	76	103	28	40	149	66	109	139	163	91	142
Schenectady	4		2	16	1	11	8		9	2	3	5
Schoharie	29	27	33	19	62	78	35	59	71	137	64	113
Schuyler	23	31	35	13	4	17	18	13	27	18	7	14
Seneca	3	3	7		4		6	9	4	10	1	10
St. Lawrence	756	832	442	331	701	1,695	822	1,352	2,308	2,496	1,091	3,032
Steuben	81	120	73	47	78	196	145	72	99	150	25	45
Sullivan	134	118	134	164	262	292	198	197	209	166	108	232
Tioga	17	19	9		2	43	27	35	16	25	21	20
Tompkins	14	9	8			25	18	7	24	21	9	
Ulster	72	23	58	23	82	65	26	130	63	63	33	115
Warren	162	266	176	80	125	184	138	228	231	341	167	340
Washington	36	21	32					54	59	25	54	134
Wayne	25	42	20	29	43	116	45	85	56	69	28	26
Westchester										1		
Wyoming	30	44	33	20	20	51	42	31				
Yates	5	12				6	17	20	25	25	6	21
Statewide	6,721	6,301	4,863	2,840	5,647	12,417	7,492	8,143	10,443	12,178	6,636	12,336

Appendix 1. NY Trapper Harvest of Beavers by County (Continued)

County	1980	1981	1982	1983	1984	1985	1986	1987	1988	1989	1990	1991
Albany	182	77	56	70	64	72	79	123	203	102	87	87
Allegany	416	446	355	701	642	1,014	247	840	654	461	396	323
Broome	108	76	43	105	52	82	110	482	288	372	190	158
Cattaraugus	497	382	439	807	543	1,216	306	947	553	595	399	338
Cayuga	140	89	43	126	51	75	109	188	149	151	65	42
Chautauqua	262	3134	252	635	462	674	152	766	532	340	432	264
Chemung	77	95	17	16	60	30			137	135	93	57
Chenango	166	114	64	152	136	227	237	615	269	449	262	163
Clinton	506	634	240	446	336	434	473	887	692	464	707	395
Columbia	132	104	12	21	20	12	31	71	106	128	69	105
Cortland	92	64	24	48	70	88	125	295	158	268	102	53
Delaware	435	311	187	185	57	131	352	561	456	223	398	336
Dutchess	122	58	55	45	69	91	190	213	159	62	106	69
Erie	39	46	58	97	40	101	22	155	45	92	45	67
Essex	712	641	219	528	400	465	583	650	708	562	525	424
Franklin	914	979	436	788	575	897	921	1,222	1,178	582	1,029	771
Fulton	361	504	182	372	196	390	255	333	411	298	126	161
Genesee	11	12		13		21		78	1	81	6	28
Greene	264	191	131	133	81	103	170	148	150	89	112	163
Hamilton	1,023	686	365	495	493	618	627	932	626	480	545	403
Herkimer	757	453	271	595	488	662	360	452	576	355	381	261
Jefferson	1,187	842	372	560	357	855	916	1,130	912	858	1,422	824
Lewis	1,812	1,013	715	1,226	1,029	1,159	1,141	2,002	1,386	875	1,796	957
Livingston	42	43	10	25	20	25		41	59	63	61	51
Madison	176	80	68	55	86	144	230	311	177	255	155	112
Monroe	23	3		22		7		42	5	32	5	9
Montgomery	133	9	5	22	42	34	12	54	88	100	59	118
Niagara		13		6						26	8	9
Oneida	378	223	150	230	193	383	227	379	474	427	356	383
Onondaga	93	62	52	47	82	39	83	167	117	191	131	175
Ontario	43	62	38	76	41	45	27	43	56	49	61	21
Orange	120	47	50	22	23	36	33	60	91	73	75	120
Orleans	4	7				2		6		17		1
Oswego	467	342	211	304	148	354	350	649	622	582	795	332
Otsego	456	437	266	125	133	133	329	930	553	474	667	490
Putnam	3	1	1	2			1	2				9
Rensselaer	158	164	106	105	21	147	74	148	117	118	64	31
Rockland	2	4				5						1
Saratoga	220	216	121	191	215	189	150	304	496	276	301	322
Schenectady	21	2	3	1	7		21	21	37	33	22	21
Schoharie	264	132	98	107	38	94	181	364	370	262	223	173
Schuyler	42	39	22	71	26	21	4	4	153	67	62	53
Seneca	7	1	15	19	8	14	10	23	46	33	18	
St. Lawrence	3,336	2,641	1,598	2,708	1,486	2,321	4,634	4,938	5,253	3,709	5,427	2,846
Steuben	172	133	104	146	134	157			572	430	313	194
Sullivan	582	315	249	164	149	345	294	311	426	366	430	366
Tioga	69	72	66	89	75	135	83	230	111	189	102	83
Tompkins	41	29	34	51	31	34	46	159	98	61	62	51
Ulster	265	158	88	79	58	121	141	226	218	139	193	130
Warren	533	441	214	309	280	374	200	395	518	399	359	363
Washington	105	185	78	116	134	213	105	218	408	241	146	145
Wayne	124	67	49	60	42	21	108	262	230	114	112	27
Westchester		1				3					4	
Wyoming	136	94	95	145	72	241	30	349	214	141	94	112
Yates	16	16	21	44	24	22	1	14	34	48	51	28
Statewide	18,246	14,169	8,349	13,914	9,789	15,080	14,958	23,754	21,892	16,645	19,645	13,223

Appendix 1. NY Trapper Harvest of Beavers by County (Continued)

County	1992	1993	1994	1995	1996	1997	1998	1999	2000	2001	2002
Albany	103	67	84	174	95	181	171	107	155	50	126
Allegany	372	365	377	774	591	683	527	242	355	254	414
Broome	266	170	305	396	258	386	370	116	93	122	175
Cattaraugus	529	337	348	614	333	849	626	312	276	215	546
Cayuga	126	49	73	213	198	166	223	117	96	45	333
Chautauqua	471	248	259	815	452	900	546	291	247	274	452
Chemung	90	73	80	163	79	208	187	58	90	55	289
Chenango	218	252	516	409	536	621	458	433	311	241	658
Clinton	555	341	436	665	853	867	366	364	441	314	514
Columbia	80	65	88	153	195	273	251	114	114	75	264
Cortland	165	170	170	253	179	274	295	143	100	112	317
Delaware	247	281	406	522	300	562	405	200	299	170	425
Dutchess	178	178	251	424	233	493	362	153	299	176	265
Erie	134	81	61	160	46	197	201	43	49	33	93
Essex	519	347	630	632	416	849	482	683	788	355	468
Franklin	679	497	968	1,552	1,569	1,936	1,025	681	1,234	711	1,298
Fulton	310	157	243	279	155	311	330	238	265	138	185
Genesee	67	32	40	39	23	46	122	69	77	27	72
Greene	81	53	84	164	76	165	128	95	72	38	101
Hamilton	470	246	530	517	284	489	540	347	375	296	318
Herkimer	456	215	406	597	383	563	401	472	326	290	490
Jefferson	836	1,105	1,618	2,473	2,128	1,864	1,619	1,133	1,446	1,139	1,328
Lewis	1,103	1,084	1,526	2,138	2,432	1,819	1,363	823	1,483	660	986
Livingston	61	42	60	117	35	56	81	61	57	26	79
Madison	179	186	242	396	251	241	233	248	224	138	358
Monroe	31	35	7	44	35	48	71	27	27	43	68
Montgomery	114	52	39	118	92	157	48	25	42	107	101
Niagara	5	15	11	5	4	10	7	14	1	11	4
Oneida	436	462	735	1,062	625	668	650	596	670	479	870
Onondaga	200	55	185	264	100	270	239	177	146	101	243
Ontario	72	70	33	82	38	85	113	53	45	13	68
Orange	52	55	70	208	110	200	317	107	121	99	197
Orleans	11	2	6	6	7	7	11	4	2	2	23
Oswego	802	323	1,237	1,342	954	805	810	817	717	580	1,210
Otsego	446	259	632	999	743	970	557	206	616	306	566
Putnam	1	1	3	9	1	14	18	9	10	17	2
Rensselaer	53	63	142	179	139	294	179	135	164	107	237
Rockland					2	2	5	11	5	11	1
Saratoga	262	299	267	493	297	424	293	284	364	206	316
Schenectady	24	14	9	43	39	47	8	35	24	12	51
Schoharie	124	98	231	436	263	410	327	198	134	100	237
Schuyler	73	46	64	142	67	77	75	28	81	58	114
Seneca	30	10	9	62	42	123	33	26	15	15	36
St. Lawrence	3,234	3,381	5,831	8,139	9,048	8.008	5,579	2,579	4,858	3,345	5,105
Steuben	380	225	268	673	254	596	457	2129	195	229	398
Sullivan	222	269	213	484	265	390	370	172	249	99	319
Tioga	212	172	213	278	184	195	249	190	119	59	173
Tompkins	65	44	50	93	29	161	122	84	34	21	66
Ulster	132	91	106	330	123	398	245	73	178	148	336
Warren	290	264	264	472	195	518	474	209	351	308	339
Washington	194	190	427	601	337	534	390	285	258	284	428
Wayne	77	78	94	203	280	370	216	40	94	43	255
Westchester	3				8	9	16			11	2
Wyoming	102	60	131	163	151	234	115	102	58	53	182
Yates	45	16	30	42	30	63	43	18	14	19	35
Statewide	15,982	13,544	21,107	31,611	26,556	31,075	23,382	14,266	18,864	12,809	22,533

Appendix 1. NY Trapper Harvest of Beavers by County (Continued)

County	2003	2004	2005	2006	2007	2008	2009	2010
Albany	42	133	101	92	241	105	128	149
Allegany	144	177	301	563	592	360	109	225
Broome	50	214	196	358	331	256	174	154
Cattaraugus	348	171	269	513	661	481	118	277
Cayuga	44	69	148	163	282	143	56	103
Chautauqua	238	418	335	595	717	516	214	351
Chemung	21	71	57	143	126	119	65	106
Chenango	238	320	327	843	421	396	207	397
Clinton	318	408	617	509	790	227	790	418
Columbia	154	202	254	189	273	155	139	235
Cortland	89	205	166	358	249	196	211	156
Delaware	205	236	201	275	288	263	315	217
Dutchess	126	196	284	216	325	133	119	98
Erie	34	88	68	54	144	92	182	41
Essex	366	419	566	664	502	452	453	440
Franklin	660	847	823	1,032	880	607	599	670
Fulton	137	219	286	302	324	222	213	203
Genesee	19	30	54	46	130	37	95	25
Greene	86	52	130	119	127	149	85	71
Hamilton	147	290	383	469	413	379	369	346
Herkimer	210	364	404	614	566	410	378	452
Jefferson	547	1,207	999	1,448	1,372	874	1,027	1,101
Lewis	466	761	978	1,061	1,276	875	1,008	1,448
Livingston	44	54	49	144	129	91	58	76
Madison	179	327	383	381	525	268	303	223
Monroe	45	30	52	47	107	10	42	39
Montgomery	47	45	89	71	105	14	108	85
Niagara	2	24	3	8	16	2	19	9
Oneida	419	730	533	1,033	757	662	710	561
Onondaga	89	213	175	331	332	277	211	144
Ontario	41	35	33	64	211	49	103	29
Orange	87	159	161	172	265	88	127	90
Orleans	1		22	8	17	14	5	4
Oswego	517	736	660	1,047	1,288	774	835	857
Otsego	424	462	515	532	559	267	402	270
Putnam	1	24	2	23	50		12	11
Rensselaer	98	163	118	159	227	182	177	105
Rockland	4			6	5			1
Saratoga	136	223	260	355	482	178	220	264
Schenectady	5	2		21	35	18	2	1
Schoharie	107	144	176	297	416	213	282	139
Schuyler	50	51	47	129	72	64	71	54
Seneca	13	43	10	29	89	35	41	52
St. Lawrence	2,353	4,305	4,023	4,884	4,528	2,417	3,674	2,985
Steuben	158	170	174	421	408	319	214	255
Sullivan	166	240	167	173	282	147	93	89
Tioga	65	208	182	242	242	153	107	70
Tompkins	39	70	76	124	178	53	54	50
Ulster	173	160	148	218	317	145	162	185
Warren	128	260	230	286	253	252	215	304
Washington	190	170	256	412	370	192	267	410
Wayne	98	57	103	132	329	278	240	71
Westchester					3		8		1
Wyoming	48	99	76	78	250	133	158	82
Yates	3	3	14	33	104	58	46	5
Statewide	10,419	16,504	16,685	22,490	23,928	15,088	16,032	15,204

Appendix 1. NY Trapper Harvest of Beavers by County (Continued)

APPENDIX II

BEAVER MANAGEMENT STATISTICS

YEAR	Beaver Harvest	Number Trappers	Beaver Problems	Mean Pelt Value	Total Value
1924&25	5,000	No Data Kept	No Data Kept	$40.00**	$200,000
1934	3,934	" " "	" " "	NDA	NDA
1935	2,498	" " "	" " "	"	"
1936	No Season	No Season	" " "	"	"
1937	2,014	848	" " "	"	"
1938	2,639	867	" " "	"	"
1939	No Season	No Season	" " "	"	"
1940	" " "	" " "	" " "	"	"
1941	3,055	1,251	" " "	"	"
1942	4,075	1,451	159	"	"
1943	2,152	672	No Data Kept	"	"
1944	3,138	1,097	" " "	$27.50***	$86,295
1945	3,275	899	" " "	NDA	NDA
1946	5,567	1,864	151	"	"
1947	No Season	No Season	210	"	"
1948	1,734	1,734	254	"	"
1949	1,966	869	327	"	"
1950	3,034	1,364	373	"	"
1951	6,002	1,895	475	"	"
1952	6,731	1,891	399	"	"
1953	9,194	1,903	329	"	"
1954	5,826	1,478	364	"	"
1955	7,649	1777	NDA	$17.00****	$130,033
1956	6,351	1,451	"	$13.00	$82,563
1957	6,768	1,539	361	$13.00	$87,984
1958	7,056	1,370	431	$15.00	$105,840
1958-59	6,047	1,436	303	$23.00	$139,081
1959-60	9,429	1,948	367	NDA	NDA
1960-61	No Pelt Tagging	No Pelt Tagging	NDA	"	"
1961-62	" " "	" " "	"	$12.00	"
1962-63	" " "	" " "	"	$14.00	"
1963-64	" " "	" " "	"	$14.00	"
1964-65	" " "	" " "	"	$11.00	"
1965-66	2,622*	492	"	$16.00	"
1966-67	5,110	922	"	$14.00	$71,540
1967-68	6,721	988	"	$17.00	$114,257
1968-69	6,301	1,197	"	$21.00	$132,321
YEAR	Beaver Harvest	Number Trappers	Beaver Problems	Mean Pelt Value	Total Value
1969-70	4,863	1,021	"	$15.00	$72,945
1970-71	2,840	584	"	$18.00	$51,120
1971-72	5,647	882	"	$22.77	$128,582
1972-73	12,419	1,672	"	$18.75	$232,856
1973-74	7,492	1,312	"	$20.80	$155,834
1974-75	8,143	NDA	706	$16.30	$133,106
1975-76	10,443	"	NDA	$22.10	$230,812
1976-77	12,178	"	"	$27.80	$338,548
1977-78	6,636	"	"	$20.30	$134,711
1978-79	12,336	"	"	$32.92	$406,101

Appendix 2. Beaver Management Statistics

Year	Beaver Harvest	Number Trappers	Beaver Problems	Mean Pelt Value	Total Value
1979-80	18,246	NDA	NDA	$31.26*****	$570,370
1980-81	14,169	2,271	"	$20.72	$293,582
1981-82	8,349	1,596	"	$14.30	$119,391
1982-83	13,914	1,849	"	$11.11	$154,585
1983-84	9,789	1,034	1,613	$14.15	$138,814
1984-85	15,080	1,618	1,546	$15.40	$232,232
1985-86	14,958	1,553	1,631	$23.00	$344,034
1986-87	23,754	2,337	1,616	$24.05	$571,284
1987-88	21,892	2,405	1,583	$20.18	$441,781
1988-89	16,645	1,694	1,648	$14.77	$249,953
1989-90	19,645	1,576	1,977	$14.05	$275,970
1990-91	13,223	1,085	1,674	$9.28	$122,709
1991-92	15,982	1,396	2,137	$11.13	$177,880
1992-93	13,544	1,101	2,113	$9.88	$133,814
1993-94	21,107	1,281	2,404	$16.37	$345,522
1994-95	31,611	1,840	2079	$17.99	$568,682
1995-96	26,556	2,275	2,395	$16.41	$435,784
1996-97	31,075	1,363	2,111	$24.13	$637,178
1997-98	23,382	2,127	2,186	$20.20	$472,316
1998-99	14,266	1,242	2,125	$12.82	$182,890
1999-00	18,864	1,040	2,156	$14.37	$271,076
2000-01	12,809	849	1,708	$18.58	$237,991
2001-02	22,533	1397	1,920	$14.41	$324,701
2002-03	10,419	875	1,922	$12.20	$127,112
2003-04	16,304	1,140	1,932	$15.01	$244,723
2004-05	16,685	1,160	1,975	$15.45	$257,783

Appendix 2. Beaver Management Statistics (continued)

*- 1965-66 pelt sealing required for only a few counties in the state.

**- 1920's pelt value taken from 16th and 32nd Annual Report of NY Conservation Department.

***- 1940's The Adirondack Record – Elizabethtown Post 4/6/1944, $70 for XXXL pelt reported, average extrapolated by proportional reduction from highest value to average value reported in Fur Auction Results, Genesee Valley Trappers Association, 2012-2013.

****- 1950's, 1960's, 1970's pelt values taken from Henry Hilton 1986. Beaver Assessment. Maine Department of Inland Fisheries and Wildlife, Bangor, ME, USA. Data from NH Fur auctions and ME Fur buyer reports.

*****1980's, 1990's, 2000's pelt values taken from Robert F. Gotie 1980 -2005. Unpublished data for New York. NY DEC, Region 7, Bureau of Wildlife, Cortland, NY, USA.

Beaver Harvest and Number of trappers from the Fur Project , Albany, NY